Writing for Nothing

Martin Crimp was born in 1956. His play *Attempts on Her Life* (1997) established his international reputation. His other work for theatre includes *When We Have Sufficiently Tortured Each Other*, *Men Asleep*, *The Rest Will be Familiar to You from Cinema*, *In the Republic of Happiness*, *Play House*, *The City*, *Fewer Emergencies*, *Cruel and Tender*, *The Country*, *The Treatment*, *Getting Attention*, *No One Sees the Video*, *Play with Repeats*, *Dealing with Clair* and *Definitely the Bahamas*. He is also the author of three texts, *Into the Little Hill*, *Written on Skin* and *Lessons in Love and Violence*, for operas by George Benjamin. His many translations of French plays include works by Genet, Ionesco, Koltès, Marivaux and Molière.

also by Martin Crimp

PLAYS ONE
(*Dealing with Clair, Play with Repeats,
Getting Attention, The Treatment*)

PLAYS TWO
(*No One Sees the Video, The Misanthrope,
Attempts on Her Life, The Country*)

PLAYS THREE
(*Cruel and Tender, Fewer Emergencies,
The City, Play House, Definitely the Bahamas,
In the Republic of Happiness*)

THE HAMBURG PLAYS
(*The Rest Will Be Familiar to You from Cinema*
and *Men Asleep*)

WHEN WE HAVE SUFFICIENTLY
TORTURED EACH OTHER

THREE ATTEMPTED ACTS
(in *Best Radio Plays of 1985*)

translations

THE CHAIRS (Ionesco)
RHINOCEROS (Ionesco)
THE MISANTHROPE (Molière)
ROBERTO ZUCCO (Koltès)
THE MAIDS (Genet)
THE TRIUMPH OF LOVE (Marivaux)
THE FALSE SERVANT (Marivaux)
THE SEAGULL (Chekhov)
PAINS OF YOUTH (Bruckner)

texts for music

INTO THE LITTLE HILL
WRITTEN ON SKIN
LESSONS IN LOVE AND VIOLENCE

MARTIN CRIMP

Writing for Nothing

with an introduction by the author

FABER & FABER

This collection first published in 2019
by Faber and Faber Limited
74–77 Great Russell Street
London WC1B 3DA

Typeset by Country Setting, Kingsdown, Kent CT14 8ES
Printed and bound in Great Britain
by CPI Group (UK) Ltd, Croydon CR0 4YY

A CIP record for this book is available from the British Library

ISBN 978-0-571-35400-9

2 4 6 8 10 9 7 5 3 1

Contents

Introduction, vii

WRITING IN PROSE

The Play, 3
Stage Kiss, 41

WRITING FOR THEATRE

Party, 51
In the Valley, 61
The Iron Rice Bowl, 73
Vaclav and Amelia, 85
The Art of Painting, 107
Advice to Iraqi Women, 115
Messenger of Love, 123

WRITING FOR MUSIC

Into the Little Hill, 141
Written on Skin, 157
Lessons in Love and Violence, 191

Writing for Nothing

When you begin writing, you write – from necessity –
for nothing. You don't expect anything in return, and
you don't get anything either, not for many years, unless
it's your own satisfaction. Decades later you will discover
the Chinese concept of 'the iron rice bowl' – similar
but not quite the same as 'job for life' – and of course
accepting this perpetual bowl of rice, especially as an
artist, means accepting to be controlled. So while it is
good and fair to be paid to write, a virtue in fact, to work
hard and be paid for it, it's nonetheless reasonable to be
wary of the effect of money, even quite small quantities,
and to remember that most writers – not that you are one
of them, really you're pretty fortunate – write and will
go on writing for what, essentially, amounts to nothing –
with the advantage of keeping the impulse pure.

How glorious it would be to begin your introduction in
this way! To raise the spectre of this ideal artistic non-
instrumental nothing – pitch up in your first paragraph
like Noah in his ark on Ararat, the irritating mass of
humanity conveniently destroyed, and, while the dove
goes flapping off looking for plant life, seize the moral
high ground!

Not so: these short texts are as grubby as all writing –
whether fiction, plays, or designed for opera. Most have
been paid for, only a few have not. Some, it has to be
said, verge on the exquisite – especially when set in the
gleaming armature of music. Others, let's admit it, have
all the allure of body-parts.

But – seriously now – is there not some hope the writer may, well once in a while at least, still write for the ideal nothing? – that he or she might once in a while at least remember that first pure impulse? – fall back in love with what he or she makes, just like the sculptor in the fable, and – if I might put it this way – head once again no place for no reason other than the word?

MC
November 2018

WRITING IN PROSE

The Play

When I heard the play read, it turned my stomach, but later that night I couldn't stop thinking about it. The writer was a little bitch, that much was obvious. I'm sick to the teeth of people who make their work so personal – and you could see it all there in the play – these characters were people she knew – the businessman who unzips his trousers and forces that girl's head down was clearly her own father – you don't need to be a psychologist to work that out. And if you want my opinion the girl is her, down on her knees, down on her knees with tears in her eyes. Okay, we know these things happen, but is this really what we want to see in the theatre? – particularly when you bear in mind that over the next sixty or ninety minutes or whatever things degenerate to the point where I would draw the line at describing them. People these days think that any kind of personal sickness or private abuse entitles them to be an artist, they think that art is simply a transcription of what they've suffered – not only that, but their own suffering completely fills the frame. If a woman has been raped by her father, if a young man has had a bad experience in prison, or at the hands of the police, then they think they have the right to reconstruct the world (and what is a play if not the rebuilding of the world?) around this event. Politics and history are made invisible. What we see on stage essentially are people of either sex being fucked up the arse. And while this happens I always notice a strange silence in the audience – a terrible gravity.

After the reading there's a similar silence, then a little applause. The actors close their scripts, take their coats off

3

the backs of the chairs, drink from water-bottles, check for messages. It's not a public reading, but one held behind closed doors, allegedly for the benefit of the writer, but in reality to give the theatre management a chance to assess a script they're undecided about. This is why despite the superficial informality of these events – cups on the floor, smiles between friends – the atmosphere afterwards is always slightly tense, fraught with judgement.

Outside in the corridor the Director asks for my opinion.

— I think it needs more work.

— More work?

— I think it's trying too hard to shock the audience.

— What about the language?

— It's confused. One moment it's brutal, the next it's romantic.

— Isn't that what makes it exciting?

— Produce the play as it is and you'll be taking an enormous risk.

— We're here to take enormous risks, says the Director, a little artificially, as the focus of his eyes adjusts so that he's looking over my shoulder.

He takes hold of my arm and lowers his voice:

— I respect your doubts, he says, but the fact is is we're going to do this play.

— Without making changes?

— It's a brilliant piece.

— I think you're making a mistake.

Our conversation stops completely at this point because the writer has appeared beside us. The Director takes her arm exactly as he took mine – except hers, as a special mark of favour, he strokes a few times, close to the shoulder. I've always found the instant physical intimacy of the theatre repellent – which isn't to say I haven't occasionally benefited from it.

— Well done, he says, stroking her arm. I think it's a wonderful piece. Shocking of course, but what I hadn't

4

realised when I first read it was just how beautiful and redeeming it is.

— It's not meant to be beautiful, she says with a smile, it's meant to be ugly.

— In that case, I say, you've clearly succeeded.

When she looks at me, there's an appalling clarity in her eyes. Something's burning there, just as there was something burning in the play. Where does this self-confidence come from? Normally if a young writer was discussing with the Director and myself the reading of their first play, she'd be looking for reassurance and advice. We'd feel a gratifying sense of responsibility and power. But in her case it's different. We're the ones being judged by this quiet burning arrogance – or at least that's what she wants us to feel. And all this does is confirm my suspicion – and she can stare as much as she likes, her eyes can burn and burn – because all this does is confirm my original suspicion that she is not a writer at all. This play of hers – which is like a living body being slowly stripped of its skin – simply represents a public act of self-mutilation.

— How d'you mean, she says, succeeded?

— In being ugly. It seems to me that despite what Nicky says no one is redeemed. Your characters live in hell.

— Is that a compliment?

— On the contrary: I'm afraid it's a criticism. Once you reach hell, no change is possible. And if no change is possible, there's no drama.

— No drama.

She grins.

— No.

— You obviously don't live in hell then.

— I've no wish to.

— Because I do – and there's plenty of fucking drama, believe me.

The Director laughs and strokes her arm.

She lights a cigarette.

— Plenty.

5

I'm always surprised that the cigarette – delivered by the slick machinery of capitalism: produced by the cheapest possible labour, sold at the highest possible price to the most vulnerable consumer – can still be worn like this as a badge of rebellion. But when she holds out the pack – a strange gesture when I've been so deliberately hostile – I can't resist taking one.

I bend towards the flame she offers me, feeling like a badly written character, not sure of my intentions.

That night I had a dream. You could call it erotic, except that word suggests pleasure, and there was none. I was shut in the dark in a shallow cupboard behind a wall. I could hear a bird flapping its wings, knocking itself against the door. The person I was with was a typical dream-person: very clear in the dream, but in reality impossible to identify. The bird went on scraping and struggling: its beak struck sparks against the surface of the door, which made me realise it must be made of metal, steel perhaps.

I woke up and was relieved to see a faint frame of light around the closed curtain. It was five o'clock. I found Madeleine in the kitchen.

— What are you doing here? I said.

— You were thrashing around. I couldn't sleep.

— I had a nightmare.

— Oh? she said. Was I in it?

She presented this as a witticism and left it to me to savour the underlying bitterness. She was smiling though, and took off the reading-glasses she knows I hate.

— I'm sorry if I woke you up.

— I think I was awake already. After all, it's summer.

This sounded quite reasonable, as if she was used to getting up at dawn, like a peasant.

— Have you fed the pigs?

She looked at me: she didn't seem to be following my train of thought. This was odd, because normally she could

read my mind with horrible clarity. She was supposed to
say 'What pigs?' which would be the cue to elaborate my
rural conceit. Instead she said:
— Are you alright?
— Why?
— You look strange.
— I feel fine.
— You look tense round your eyes.
What she was doing, of course, was trying to shift the
attention on to me. Because I didn't look remotely strange
– what was strange, as she well knew, was her sitting there
in the kitchen at five o'clock in the morning when it was
quite normal for her to still be in bed at ten o'clock or even
midday.
She was right about summer, though. The sun streamed
in from the east and raked across the piles of junk: the
books, the postcards, the scripts, the leftovers, the crumbs
on the table, the knife in the jam-jar. It would soon be un-
pleasantly hot because there were no blinds on the tall windows, which were spattered on the outside by the weather
and on the inside by cooking fat. On the window-ledge a
comb with hair in it threw a long tangled shadow. I said:
— We should clear some of this stuff up.
— What stuff?
— Well that pile of magazines.
— I'm keeping them. I need them.
— We could put them somewhere else. We could file
them.
— File them?
I've managed to make her laugh. This means the day
will be bearable.

But don't be taken in by the squalor. The squalor in which
Madeleine and myself live is purely cosmetic. Underneath
the crumbs and stains is a solid and valuable property
in one of the city's most desirable districts. Sitting here

quietly on my own sometimes I feel the value of the house thickening around me until it starts to press against my ear-drums. I'd like to say that I was the one who resisted this gift, that it was me who foresaw the poisonous nature of so much security, but the fact is I was all for it, and completely failed to understand why Madeleine opposed her father's generosity. It wasn't as if his money was tainted. He produced commercial comedies and musical entertainments in theatres inherited from his own father: hardly exploitation. He was rich but benign. And like the kind of plays he produced, there was something harmless – appealing, even – about his shallowness. Compared to my own parents, with their bottled fruit, their home-grown salad, roast meat on Sundays and cold meat on Mondays, deference to doctors, bedtime prayers, grace before meals – compared to their suburban intuition that life was inherently difficult and shameful, Madeleine's father seemed to imply that on the contrary life was simply a series of presents waiting to be unwrapped. Why shouldn't we accept the house?

— I don't want to give him that satisfaction.

— What satisfaction?

— The satisfaction of putting us in his debt.

— I'm sure he doesn't see it that way.

— You don't know anything about my father. All you see is the surface.

— As far as your father's concerned the surface is all there is.

— My father doesn't invest money without expecting a return. He's a businessman.

— He's also your father. The only investment he wants to make is in our future. A parent doesn't expect what you call 'a return' from his own child, Madeleine.

I hope our dialogue wasn't that stilted, but I suspect it was. It's only years of marriage that have honed our conversations into something altogether more subtle and hurtful. At the time, though, Madeleine started to cry, which put an end – perhaps intentionally – to any rational

8

debate. Her tears were confusing. You have to remember how beautiful she was, and how vulnerable she could look. When she cried her face didn't collapse the way it does now, it became even more desirable. Usually her tears led to us making love, and there's nothing more exquisite than making love to a woman in tears because – and this is particularly gratifying for a man – she becomes emotionally naked. This is why I reached out to put my arms around her. I imagined I would kiss away those tears. So I was surprised when she pushed me back with her fists and said 'Don't fucking touch me' in a tight, bitter voice I was hearing for the first time.

We were in the country. It was Berkshire. She'd walked a little way towards the stream and turned her back to me. Beyond the stream are two horses – chestnuts – cropping the grass. In the distance I can now hear the empty crack of a shotgun, but at the time I heard nothing because Madeleine filled the whole frame of my feelings, and occupied all of my senses. Her hair hung down her back like a curtain of black, brown and gold, excluding me. We might've looked like a woodcut by Munch: two still, emblematic figures, distress eddying away from us across the landscape in red and green spirals – if it hadn't been Berkshire.

The dull thudding across the meadow was Madeleine's father coming towards us, his puppet-like stride explained by the steep slope. He'd left those bright tiny figures on the terrace – actors? dancers? – to come down and find us. He was a little breathless, and had spilled some of his drink on the sleeve of his blazer.

— Well? he said. Is it yes or is it no? John?

— We're still talking about it, I said.

— No we're not. Madeleine turned and smiled. We'd love to have the house, Daddy. It's the most wonderful wedding-present we could think of.

Although she hadn't touched her face, there was no trace of tears, only a white mask of serenity. Our country-house melodrama appeared to have ended.

— Well I'm absolutely delighted for you both. Because I know I can be a bit of a prick sometimes, but just because a man's a bit of a prick doesn't mean you have to treat him like a cunt, does it John.

— No one's treating you like a cunt, Daddy.

— I'm asking John.

— He doesn't understand what you mean.

— Are you trying to tell me my future son-in-law doesn't know the difference between a prick and a cunt?

— Can't we just stop now. We'd love to have the house. We're both very grateful.

— Because if he doesn't know the difference I'm not sure I want him marrying my most precious daughter.

— Your only daughter.

— Only and most precious. Well does he?

— Does he what?

— Does he know the difference? John?

— You're embarrassing him.

— Because I'll tell you something, Johnny-boy, this daughter of mine is no job for amateurs.

All three of us laughed, although the exchange of obscenities had left me feeling prudish and suburban. We walked together up the slope towards the actors and dancers, the lamps and the drinks.

We stayed there in the country while the house in town was prepared for us. It took a number of weeks to evict the tenants, whose children had scribbled over the walls, and inside cupboards. We tore down thin partitions to reveal perfectly proportioned rooms full of light.

— Are you alright?

— Why?

— You look strange.

— You've already said that.

Is this irritating woman hunched over the kitchen table really the girl I fell in love with? She's doing this deliberately.

— Have I?

— You know you have.

And suddenly it all falls into place: the reading-glasses, the open script, it's the play, she's reading the play. She got up at five o'clock in the morning to read the play.

— You're reading the play.

— Yes.

— Again?

— Why not again? I think it's an important piece of work.

Important? What she means – and I see it all too clearly – is that Madeleine has deluded herself into imagining that just because she took part in yesterday's reading, she'll be offered a part. This is what actors mean by 'important': *important to me.*

— Important? I hated it. The writer needs to grow up.

— You would say that.

— What's that supposed to mean?

— So what were the two of you talking about?

— The two of who?

— You and Rachel. I suppose you were taking her cigarettes and telling her how much you hated her play.

— Well as a matter of fact, that's exactly what I was doing.

— You really think she values your judgement?

— I don't think she values anyone's judgement. I think she's an arrogant little bitch.

— Oh really? And what else?

— What else what?

— Don't get your hopes up.

— What hopes?

I'd like to throw this hot coffee right in her face, but of course I simply sit at the end of the table smiling. Madeleine must be humoured. The enormity of her failure must never be forgotten. It never really worked out for her, did it, acting. Not once Daddy's influence began to decline. Not once the connection with 'Daddy' began to shut more doors than it had opened. All Madeleine ever had, let's face it, was her beauty – clear white skin, the curtain of hair, lamp-like eyes – and her presence, which she still has, naturally, even now – when she puts the glasses back on the end of her nose, and looks at me over the top of the frame, like a degenerate schoolmistress, wearing that silk nightdress or whatever it is, that used to make her body so subtle and desirable but now clings to it with the cruel precision of supermarket meat-wrapping and brings to mind that most horrible of words: slut.

— Don't hate me.

— I don't hate you, Madeleine.

— I can see it in your eyes.

And now this terrible play. Terrible because she'll set her heart on it, and be disappointed. She's always used for readings. She's always here. Waiting. She's always available. But when it comes to the performance, that's when they look for someone more fashionable, harder to get, more 'interesting' – someone better, to put it bluntly. The theatre doesn't want her any more, that's the truth. If you ever see Madeleine now, she's that psychiatric patient cutting herself in one episode of a TV drama – or if she's lucky she's sitting in an eighteenth-century drawing room, embroidering bitterly, while her niece, or her ward, or something like that, lies under the trees with a sexually voracious aristocrat. The theatre simply doesn't want her – her tired flesh, her brittle voice. But she's always here. Waiting. Too grand to wash up. Too much of an artist to take the knife out of the marmalade and put the lid back on. Too charismatic to wipe those smears off the windows or pull her own hair – great long greasy clots of it – out of the plughole in the bath – I have to hook it out with a piece of wire and flush it down the toilet. And meanwhile the niece or the ward is lying under the trees, and the head of the young aristocrat has disappeared under her skirts.

— Admit this play gets under your skin.

— I never said it doesn't have its powerful moments.

— Admit it's extraordinary, can't you. Admit that that's why we're both sitting here at half past five in the morning talking about it.

— I'm not talking about it.

— I've noticed.

— What's that supposed to mean?

— You're not talking about it because you're a man.

Oh I see. Of course. Because I'm a man.

— You're not talking about it because you feel threatened by it.

— I feel threatened? Excuse me?

That's right, Madeleine: if all else fails, let's reduce everything to some kind of unanswerable gender-based bullshit.

— Yes. Of course you do. In all sorts of ways.

— Name one.

She can't of course. Instead she takes off her glasses and stares out of the window as if she didn't hear. The sun's really quite intense now. We've been meaning to put up blinds for years. I hate the way the milk warms up in the milk bottle. And once it's warmed up even once, you can put it back in the fridge, you can use it again, but it always has that smell.

My mum and dad are standing in the hall. The parquet floor. The stairs with their mahogany stair-rail winding elegantly upwards. They look humble and a little suspicious. If my dad had a cap he'd 've doffed it and be feeding the circumference from one hand to the other like the servant with bad news in a silent movie. My mum's holding some terrifying home-grown gift. We don't touch. We don't kiss. We don't greet. It's not part of our vocabulary. Of course they would like love, but what right have they to expect love when they never taught me how to express it?

Then Madeleine appears. Kisses my father (he blushes), hugs my mother, takes the gift ('How wonderful! Thank you so much!'), removes their coats, shows them the coat closet ('Oh,' says my mum, 'someone's been scribbling on the walls.' 'Yes, isn't it sweet?' says Madeleine 'Apparently there were some children living here'), makes tea (this doesn't come naturally to Madeleine, as my mother immediately detects, looking sideways at my dad with compressed lips – how she longs to be warming that pot, counting out that tea, doing it all as it should be done), and finally unwraps the present, which turns out to be not the thick sweet marmalade I'd imagined from the weight of it, but an ugly 'crystal' vase, a fat block of glass which ten years from now I will duck, screaming, to avoid, as she hurls it at me and makes it shatter into aquamarine flakes against the bedroom wall. For the moment though, unaware of the future, she places it graciously on the table ('How lovely') and catches my eye in a way that makes me feel like the happiest human being alive.

She's pretending to be the girl-next-door. She's dressed almost like a child, with a black velvet band in her hair. I wonder what my dad makes of this? Does he ever think about sex? Does he ever wonder what it would be like to sleep with Madeleine? Lock himself in the bathroom on a Saturday afternoon? Jerk himself off in a hot bath while my mum's baking? He opens a pack of cigarettes – the more expensive brand he smokes at weekends – and lights one with his enormous hands. He doesn't have many more years to live. He'll retire and die. I'll never know what he thinks. I'll never share one thought with him, nor he a single thought with me, his only son. He looks 'approvingly' around the room through lenses as thick as the crystal vase.

— You should ask Madeleine if you can smoke, says my mum, managing to make this into a criticism not just of my father but of Madeleine as well.

— Of course he can smoke. He knows he doesn't have to ask. In fact I'll take one too, if I may.

She grabs the pack – again like a child – and my dad reaches towards her with his cheap transparent lighter – chivalrous – enchanted.

Then comes the tour. We climb floor after floor. We pass through room after room. At first my parents are amazed. Then the repetition begins to bore them, although they're careful not to show it. But by the time we reach the top landing, from the way they smile, I can tell they disapprove. After all, they're the ones who've saved, who've watched the price of potatoes, who've cut worn sheets up the middle and joined them at the edges, who've made you eat everything on your plate, then served you tinned cream and tinned pineapple as a treat, who've economised, been faithful, and died. While we're the ones who'll leave the lights burning all night, fuck who we like, put our old clothes out for the bin-men and pay for expensive meals we're too drunk to finish.

— It won't be easy to keep clean, Madeleine, says my mum.

— What's up there then? says my dad, looking at a steeper flight of plain stairs that twist into the dark.

— That's where your son goes when he wants to pretend he's a starving artist, says Madeleine.

The doorbell terrified my parents. No one ever came to our house when I was a child. No one ever 'turned up'. There were no parties. They had no friends, only one or two relatives, whose brief visits were carefully planned. That's why they froze when the bell went and tightened their lips while Madeleine ran down all those stairs to open the huge front door.

But her father (who still had a key? oh?) had already let himself in – you could hear the laughter.

— This is Hayley, he said, from Leeds.

— I'm not from Leeds, I'm from Pontefract. I keep telling him.

— But Leeds is where I discovered you.

— Now he thinks he's Christopher-fuck-me-Columbus.

— What were you doing in Leeds, Hayley?

— Hayley was acting.

— Excuse me: not just acting. I'm a real good dancer, and I can sing as well.

— Hayley does a bit of everything.

— He should be so lucky.

Everybody laughs – except my mum who's watching Hayley knock the ash from her cigarette straight into the sea-green vase. Suddenly she says:

— How old are you, Hayley? Do your parents know you're here?

— I could ask you the same question, says Hayley.

Which makes us all laugh again, all except Madeleine's father, who turns to my mother and explains that Hayley is nineteen years old, and that her parents, please don't worry, are actually family friends.

My mum's mouth is already developing the radiating lines of judgement that will one day make it look like the mouth of a drawstring bag. What's any of this got to do with her? Why can't she just shut up? Even on the way out she's still saying in a loud 'whisper' to my dad '. . . Doesn't look more than fourteen . . .' and my dad's nodding, grinning, yes, yes, anything, whatever you say, let's just go, let's just go.

The meeting's at half past ten. I've already been awake for more than five hours which is why I need a *caffè corretto* at the Italian place before I go in. The room's very small and hot. There's a big desk with the usual towers of scripts in dull manila folders. Sometimes I can't believe we come here week after week to pick our way through these piles of mediocrity – and all the hours of work they represent – all the illusions they represent – all those writers sitting at night under their lamps in their quiet circles of light, at their faint flat screens, writing page after page of flaccid, forgettable dialogue – printing it, binding it, re-reading it –

utterly indifferent to their own lack of talent. And what is that sickening smell? Stale coffee. Someone's left the machine on, but there's no water in it. It wouldn't occur to anyone here to switch it off, would it, to open a window. A few commonsense domestic reflexes wouldn't be out of place here amongst this group of script-advisors, of young assistants, literary helpers, would-be directors. Just like Madeleine in fact – not a clue – can't be bothered – let's just all sit here and suffocate, shall we? But when the window is finally opened, there's drilling in the street, right outside the building, some kind of trench, some kind of pit they're making out there, a number of men in Day-Glo jackets threatening our intellectual activity. There's nothing for it but to shut the window again and sweat.

So why when the Director arrives does he look so cool and bright? He beams round at us with his air-conditioned smile – six months ago it would've seemed sincere, but already it's tainted by power – that's why it looks strangely suspended, like a smile in a photograph. He takes his seat and now there's a little pause in which – thank God for that – the drills stop and the air can be heard bleeding out of the compressor. A girl pokes her head round the door and hands him a sheet of paper – whisper whisper whisper – he glances at it – yes yes yes – tell them we need to discuss this with New York – whisper whisper whisper – hands back the paper, the girl's gone.

— Well, he says, this has been a marvellous few days for me, and I hope no one will mind if I divert slightly from the agenda in front of you just to say one or two things about the week's developments – if that's alright with everyone here – and I assume it is.

Divert? He means deviate. I realise too late I'm sitting with my back to the sun.

— Quite a few of you came to the reading of Rachel's play yesterday, and I think all of you who were there will have felt – as I did – privileged to have witnessed an event which I truly believe is going to be a landmark in the life of this theatre. Aside from its sheer brutal energy – its daring – its power to shock and disturb – I think what the reading revealed was the underlying wit and subtlety of the writing – which I think many of us – and I'm including myself in this – had maybe underestimated. I know there had been a broad consensus that the reading would be followed by a period of further development of the text, which John here had kindly offered to lead. But my over-whelming feeling is that the play is what it is, and that we should now move to protect the writer from any input which could distort her own unique voice. What looked like faults on the page were things that the actors and my-self discovered to be absolutely accurate discontinuities of feeling – thrilling moments in a play that doesn't just move the theatrical goal-posts – it rewrites the entire rules of the game.

Despite the tired metaphor, everyone's nodding, glow-ing with a kind of corporate satisfaction. The drills begin again.

— Which is why – as some of you already know – I'm taking the unusual step of moving this piece straight into production.

I beg your pardon? Who already knows? Just what the fuck is happening here?

— We need to be brave. And we need to be bold. Is there anything we can do about that noise? Yes? No?

An assistant slips out.

— And I'm particularly thrilled to be able to say that we've managed to secure a commitment from all the actors who took part in the reading. Does anyone have any ques-tions?

— Yes, I have a number of questions.

— John?

What does he mean: *from all the actors*? Is he talking about Madeleine? Surely he means: *from all the actors except Madeleine*. What kind of slimy political manoeuvring is going on here? Some fucking bullshit arm-stroking trust-me-I'm-a-cunt deal struck in a corridor.

— John? Are you with us?

Candid black eyes. The smirk of power. Take your time, John, take your time.

— Certainly I'm with you if you mean with you in the sense of lucid. Because I have to say I feel unusually lucid this morning, despite, or perhaps because of, a particularly early start, a particularly . . . what is the word? . . . a particularly early and invigorating start to the day . . . (Laughter: he's not the only one who can make speeches.) . . . but if, Nicky, you mean with you in the sense of in agreement with a decision which with the greatest respect seems to be not just hasty but misconceived, then I have to say that no, I'm not with you at all.

— That's not a question.

— I'm sorry?

— You said you had a number of questions.

— Absolutely. And the first is: could someone spare me a cigarette?

This goes down very well – I can feel even the faint tremor as I take it working to my dramatic advantage.

— And the second is: I don't understand how this decision has been made without consulting me.

— Again, that's hardly a question, but the fact is is we talked if you remember after the reading.

— I do indeed remember. And we did indeed talk. Which is human. People talk – of course they do – we call this dialogue. And dialogue is something we all know about. Page after page. Week after week. Meaningless. All of us know – well don't we? – we all know that serious theatre, literature, cinema, is dissolving in front of us. That even the most radical gesture is sterilised by money, commodified, and like this cigarette, sold back to us as a kind of death. But we still come here and pretend we're presiding over a golden age. We pick over the latest sordid slice of

life or sick fantasy as if it were an undiscovered master-
piece by Ibsen or Aeschylus. We talk about opening up the
theatre, but we know that not one of those men digging up
the road out there will ever come through these doors to
see the bold brave work that Nicholas is talking about –
and nor in all probability will their children.

— I don't quite see what this has to do with Rachel's
play.

Of course you don't. Because you never think. Because
you're full of shit. Because you surround yourself with
people who are afraid to criticise you – just look at them all
with their heads down, doodling. Because you touch people
inappropriately. Stroke women's arms inappropriately. Sed-
uce every young girl who turns up in a short skirt looking
for a job. Because you're a child who's been given power.
Because for reasons I have yet to fully understand you
intend to cast my wife in a role of sickening degradation.

— What?

— I don't quite see, John – forgive me – what this has
to do with Rachel's play.

— Uh-huh.

— Yes.

— You don't see.

— Yes. No. I don't.

— D'you think we could open a window. Because
I came in here this morning and no one had opened a
window.

— You're right. It's terribly hot in here. Can someone
get him a glass of water.

— I don't want a glass of water.

— Okay.

— I don't need a glass of water.

— Okay. Fine. Are you alright?

Oh yes, I'm in clover. I'm lying on a soft mountain
meadow with my hand dipped in a stream of melted snow.

— Excuse me.

— John?

It's coming up into my throat. There's nothing I can do about it.

— Excuse me. I'll be straight back.

— Don't worry. Take your time.

— It's the heat.

— We understand.

— I'm coming straight back.

— That's fine. We'll wait. Someone open the door for him.

— I can manage, thank you.

The door is not the problem. Don't give me that compassionate bollocks. You are the problem. And the body. This human body – this flesh – which contains both heaven and hell.

Why am I afraid to go down the little wooden stairs? I tidy my papers. I switch off the lamp. I stand behind my door like a child at night who wants to see his parents but wonders if they'll be angry. What am I frightened of? It's 'my' house. It's 'my' wife. Some time after eleven they come swarming in from the Strindberg. You can hear them shrieking in the hall. Then the music begins to beat up through the floors. (The way the paper cones of the speakers pulse in and out – who'd've believed the physical displacement could be so visible, so immense?) They drink and dance. They smoke and cook – eggs, toast, spaghetti – everything sticks, everything burns. Who cares how much she drinks. Who cares who she dances with. I'm the one she'll turn to when they're finally out – lurching into the street – when the music stops. I'm the one she'll turn to. And that's the thing that can't be acted – that giving of yourself – that giving of your body. There's no reason to be afraid, then: no reason to wait in the dark behind the door. Let her act what she likes – schoolgirl in white blouse flirting with my dad – or suicidal aristocrat fascinated by sex and death who watches the greenfinch split open on the butcher's block, and smears her face with the bird's blood.

When I've vomited I feel much better. The cubicle is calm. It's a good idea to wait here, just for a while, while the cistern refills. It's a good sound – a steady sound: as the float rises, so the valve closes.

She'd turn towards the audience wearing the blood like a mask:
— A servant's a servant.
— And a whore's a whore.
But the cruellest line she'd stolen for herself (it was Daddy's theatre, she could do what she liked):
— You were too easy to be really exciting.

It's surprisingly clean on the floor, but I can't stay here all day. In no time at all, I'm on my feet, I'm unlatching the door, I'm in the washroom where the porcelain urinals are. The light comes soft and beautiful through the ground-glass windows. It's like a pub at lunchtime after a funeral – the best time, the best light. Things are improving, oh yes. The water's cold. I use some to rinse the taste out of my mouth and some to splash my face. I work the water into my hair with my fingers. Suddenly it seems like a holiday – heat, light, water in my hair. What was it she said? 'It's summer, after all.' But when did we last lie naked listening to the sea?
— John?
When did we last stand on a terrace that burned our feet?
— John? We thought you'd gone.
— I was washing my face.
— So I see.
— What's happened to the meeting?
— Finished. We waited for you.
The enormity of that 'So I see'.

— Listen . . . I don't want you to feel that anyone's gone behind your back.

— No.

— Your opinion is very highly valued in this building.

— Yes.

— I'd be a fool not to pay attention. I'm the new boy. I'm still learning the ropes.

— Yes.

— The last thing I want to do is hurt you.

— Hurt me? How?

— In any way, John, in any way. Let me make that clear.

You've made it clear. Thank you. Can I go now? And please stop using intimacy as a tool.

— I hear you're doing a telly thing. How's it going?

— What telly thing?

— Maddy told me you were doing a telly thing.

— Madeleine?

— Some telly thing. Yes.

— I don't work for television.

— Well that's what I thought. Only Maddy told me you were.

— Madeleine's wrong. She doesn't always know what she's talking about, I'm afraid – but you've probably realised that.

He just looks at me. It's obviously never crossed his mind. This man knows nothing about the deviousness of human beings.

— I'm thrilled, actually.

— Oh? Are you?

— Thrilled – yes – to be working with Madeleine. I think she's hugely underrated. It's far too long since she was offered a leading part. You should be proud of her.

— Not since the Strindberg.

— The what?

— The Strindberg.

— Really?

23

You can see he's lost. Look at him. His eyes have tightened – as if I'm print he finds too small to read.

— Listen, he says, picking a hair off my sleeve, why don't you take a break for a few days?

— Why should I do that?

— I don't know . . . Give yourself some space. Take Madeleine to that place of yours in the country. Berkshire, isn't it?

— We don't have a place in the country.

— Yes you have. I've been there.

— We sold it.

— I didn't know that.

— There's no reason why you should.

— I'm sorry.

— It was a business decision.

— I'm sorry all the same.

— It was Madeleine's.

— The house – or the decision?

What's that supposed to mean? That I'm incapable of making decisions? That I defer to my wife? That I married for money? Or is he wondering whether her property – Daddy's gift – remains outside my control?

— We owned it jointly. It was a joint decision.

— I'm joking. Calm down.

— I'm perfectly calm.

— Calm down, John. And take a break. That's my advice. Take as long as you need. And when you're back the two of us can talk.

— We are talking.

— I mean really talk. Talk about the work.

— As long as I need.

— Exactly.

— And how long would you say that was?

— How long? That's a judgement only you can make. Listen, I have to go. I have a lunch.

One last smile, then he switches off the beam of his attention and runs up the stairs like a schoolboy.

The men are sitting on the steps in the sun, eating out of paper bags. In one pile are the broken slabs of tarmac, the crust of the street – in another, the earth. At the bottom of the deep dry pit there are pipes wrapped in rags. Television thing. What exactly has she been saying? And the play – even this morning as she was sitting there accusing me of strangeness, she already knew. She'd had the offer. She'd accepted the offer. She was basking in her secret glory like a lizard on a rock.

Everyone's clustering round the doorways of the pubs and bars. The expression is 'spilling on to the street' – but these people aren't spilling, they're seething. The pubs and bars, with their black open doorways, are like the nests of insects about to swarm. These are the relentless young, the childless young, looking for the sunshine the way an actor on stage looks for the light. What makes it so easy for them to laugh and chatter, tip back their heads, open their mouths? They look like a commercial for themselves: an image designed to sell themselves back to themselves – tip your head, open your mouth, spend money, be happy.

But this is strange: one of the insects – it's a beetle with vast black eyes – detaches itself from the wall – puts down its empty glass – detaches itself from the wall and begins moving towards me.

— Hello, it says.

My head is condensed double in the black mirrors. The beetle is amused.

— What are you doing? it says.

There's no reason why I should speak to a beetle.

— You don't remember me, do you, it says, still smiling. We met yesterday, it says.

Everything's buzzing. The world's too hot.

— We met after the reading, it says. Rachel. I'm Rachel.

You may be Rachel, but that doesn't mean I have to speak to you. Just because you're human and have a name doesn't mean I have to speak to you. If I spoke to everyone who was human, if I spoke to everyone who had a name, how would the chattering ever stop?

— I was wondering, says Rachel, what it would be like to lie down in that hole and be covered in earth.

— Oh were you?

— Yes I fucking was.

You see: this is what happens when you try and make conversation. She takes off the beetle-black glasses. Her eyes flick from side to side, examining each of mine in turn.

— I know you hate my play.

— I'm sorry? I don't remember saying that.

— Not to my face.

I beg your pardon? People don't talk like this. They are discreet, tolerant, respectful, and full of shit.

— Alright then: let's discuss it. I'll buy you a drink.

— You'll buy me a drink?

— Is that funny? Why is that funny?

— I've had a drink.

— Have another.

— I can't. Sorry. Listen . . .

But why is she placing her hand on my shoulder? – by what right? – by what right is she laying her hand like this on my shoulder and saying, 'I can't stop. I'll be late'? Her eyes flick. Finally she removes her hand, but not before she's kissed my cheek – not a theatre-kiss, but a real one in which her lips touch my skin.

(I suppose it would be cool at first – and the earth would be soft and comfortingly heavy, like a woman lying on you. But in the end it would be dark, and when you opened your mouth to scream the soil would flood right in to the root of your tongue.)

Then she's gone up the steps and into the theatre through the glass door which swings very slowly shut as the sky slides across it.

There's an art to having lunch on your own – a particular

joy. Sit at the back. Find somewhere dark. That way everything gleams. The glass gleams and the knives look as if their blades are made of mercury. The street's still visible through the window – people – sunlight – but far away, with the sound switched off. No one blocks your view – no husband, no wife, no lover, no colleague, no friend – no one mops up your attention. Your relationship is with your food, with your glass of wine, with the click of cutlery. Your conversation is with yourself. (And isn't this where God sits at lunchtimes – at the back of an inexpensive restaurant – an old man with long white hair looking guiltily at creation through the plate-glass window while he strokes the creases out of the tablecloth?)

There's something unbalanced about that girl, and they all refuse to see it. That odd bitch kiss of hers, for example – what was that supposed to mean? I can still feel it on my skin, like a dab of ether. 'Trouble' – she's what my mum and dad would've called 'trouble' – not the Madeleine kind: capricious, self-conscious – no, I'm talking about the serious kind: splinters of glass – bite-marks – blood in the sink – madness, basically. Oh yes, oh yes, it's all very well for him to sit there in his aesthetic sanctuary and talk about 'discontinuities of feeling' – to talk about being bold and brave – but the words he should really be using are 'pornography', 'despair', 'narcissism', 'psychosis'. Why not just tear out her heart, tear out the writer's heart on stage and 'drink out of her skull'?

Fuck this – what I need is a salad – something green and living – and a bottle of wine so cold it tastes of steel.

— Why are you hiding?
— I'm not hiding.
— Well open the door then.

When I opened the door, the music became not so much louder, as more exact. She stood there breathless – which was to be expected – she'd raced up three flights of stairs –

although perhaps the real reason was the obscene current
of the play still running through her.
— Why are you standing there in the dark? she said.
I tried to pull her into the room, but she resisted me.
— I can't, she said, the people from America are here.
The people from America? She was still panting. She
adjusted her dress, pulling it down over her hips. She said:
— Really, they're not as terrible as you think.
— What people from America?
— They want to talk movies.
— Talk movies?
— I told you they were coming. They want to film the
play. They want to make a film of the play. And they want
me. They want me to be in it. Isn't it incredible?
— It's totally incredible, I said.
Now I could see why she was breathless.
— It's totally incredible, I said, that anyone who 'talks
movies' would consider making a film out of Strindberg.
And it's even more incredible, I said, that anyone would
believe them.
— What?
And she obviously did. She really did believe that the
people who set the world alight with napalm, then doused
the flames with Coca-Cola, that these same people could
possibly be interested in the unprofitable micro-emotions
of turn-of-the-century Swedes, let alone make a film about
them with their disgusting bloodstained dollars.
— Please come downstairs and meet them, she said,
or it will look bad. They know you're here. They'll think
you're hiding.
— I don't like these parties.
— I know you don't. But just for tonight. Just for me.
Please. They're really not as terrible as you think.
From the fact she's said this twice, I began to get an idea
of just how terrible the people from America must be. Some-
how I could see them ballooning up the stairs towards

me – gas-filled balloons, grinning and obese, with long silver strings.

— Please. – She licked my ear. – We need the money.

The whole house was throbbing. It beat like a heart laid bare in an experiment. I thought: how strange that paper cones can make so much noise. I also thought: it's 'my' house, and so it must be 'my' heart – although I knew that wasn't true, because my own heart was packed safely away behind my ribs, where only Madeleine could touch it.

This was nothing to do with money: it was to do with vanity. It was to do with her moving image being projected onto giant screens.

— I don't like Americans, I said.

— You've never met them.

— I'm talking about their politics.

— Oh, politics, politics . . . Just come and say hello, that's all.

The house was full of men and women I'd never met. They all had that carefree look of people who are eating and drinking at someone else's expense, who are experiencing (as they let their cigarettes burn out, for example, on a surface of eighteenth-century mahogany) the unique joy of trashing someone else's property. As we got closer to the source of the music – a dark room full of ugly dancing – I found it harder and harder to hear. I couldn't understand how all around me people could go on talking. Madeleine's mouth was right next to my ear again, almost covering it. She was saying in the intensest of whispers '. . . one of the richest women in California . . .' before she squeezed my fingers and vanished.

The woman in front of me appeared to be dead. Her skin was like putty. She held out her hand, but when I gripped it, the hand didn't grip back. It was cold. The muscles felt wasted. The man beside her was more like the American of my imagination – huge, bearded – a conqueror.

The people from America began to talk: something about how wonderful something had been. How there was a great need – a great desire – an appetite for something – because what was it someone had said? – because someone had said something about something – which was so true, which was so incredibly true – was it Chekhov maybe? – one of those Russians anyway – and what an amazing thing, what an amazing thought that someone could do something – read? – write? – read or write something and then after decades – or even centuries – and then there was someone – Madeleine – there was Madeleine who was truly amazing – and I mean really and truly amazing – there was an incredible something for Madeleine – future maybe – an incredible future or something ahead of her – you could sense it – we could all sense it – hey, come on: we could all sense it sitting there in the something – the dark – the theatre – everyone could sense it – the future, the amazing future – and then the screen – doing something to the screen – transforming? – transferring – transferring it to the screen – capturing something and transferring it to the screen – transferring the amazing future to the screen, that was the task for someone – for them? – for us? – no, not for us – of course not for us – for them – for people from America – the task for people from America was to capture something – everything – to capture everything and transfer the amazing future to the screen.

   — Absolutely, I said.

   — I hope you were nice to them.

   — What?

   — I hope you were nice to them. Unzip me.

   — Of course I was nice to them.

She bowed her head to let her hair fall clear of the zip. The tight dress split open like a cellophane wrapper. The house was quiet. It would soon be light.

   — What did you say to them?

   — How d'you mean?

— You weren't rude? You didn't close any doors? Where had she learned to speak like this?

— Doors? Of course I didn't close any doors.

— Thank you.

Out in the street the first people – the people who'd slept – the people who'd put out clean breakfast bowls and set their alarms before they went to bed – the people who quite possibly dreamed of leading the exact life we were at that moment leading – the life of the theatre – were on their way to work. You could hear the brisk click of their footsteps.

— What d'you mean, I said, about the money?

— I don't want to talk about money, said Madeleine.

Underneath the dress she was – as was her habit – completely naked.

— I want you to kiss me.

The bill appears in an embossed vinyl folder. There's a word for this: leatherette. Inside the folder there's a little pocket. The pocket says: 'Place your credit card here.' The bill says: SERVICE IS NOT INCLUDED. The empty bottle says: '*Non disperdere il vetro nell'ambiente*' – Don't throw (disperse) glass into the ambience (the environment, the outside world). Two arrows interlocking in a circle imply that the bottle will be melted down and turned into other bottles, saving us from extinction: and the more we drink, the more we will be saved.

The afternoon's radiant. It's the kind of afternoon when you can believe that light's made of particles. In fact you can see them streaming down from the sun like pollen. How many times I must've made this walk – from the house to the theatre, from the theatre to the house. All the shops have changed. They used to sell the things we need: fish, fruit, thread – now they sell shoes, scented candles, and stainless-steel 'professional' cookware for people who have no time to cook.

The house next door has changed hands, too. The labyrinth of bed-sits was stripped out, the way ours once was. Now there's a single doorbell, and behind that small glinting square of glass, the lens of a camera. The man has a very pink face. He told me his name was Richard and that we were neighbours. He travels a lot and has the happy confidence of a man who has been serviced by prostitutes in a number of different time-zones. This is his right, since he's clearly the 'provider'. I don't know what the woman's called. Sometimes I see her bring out her child and strap it into a military-looking vehicle with enormous wheels. The child is very quiet and wary: already it suspects it should never have been born.

The effect has been to make our own house look shabby, quite frankly. Even in this most flattering, most golden of lights, there's no hiding the flaking and cracking. It needs scaffolding. It needs a couple of men in white overalls – not kids who don't give a toss – but older men with families and a bit of humility. It needs those ladders with wheels – roof-ladders – that roll up the slates and hitch over the ridge – someone to sort out the flashing, the pointing on the chimney-stack, rake out the crumbling mortar, replace the lead.

The front door still opens easily enough. The hall's still wide and cool. Let's deal with this calmly and rationally, shall we.

— Madeleine?

There's a murmur in the first big drawing room, but it's the TV. The sun's shining on the screen, bleaching the colour out of it. I switch it off and pick up the little cluster of mugs she always leaves where she's been sitting. Straightening up, I catch sight of myself in the antique mirror: in the stained silver I look like a character from the past – the servant.

— Madeleine?

I put the mugs with the other debris on the kitchen table, which is where I find the note: 'Dubbing. Back later. Love, Madeleine xx' This note has a number of unusual features – the x's – the breathless punctuation – the use of 'love'.

— Madeleine? Are you here?

What exactly does she mean? The full stops betray a kind of repellent excitement – haste, purpose. And does she really imagine that those x's are anything other than marks on a page? As for love, the word drops like a stone down a mine-shaft, never reaching the bottom.

Then she's home – bustling in – clattering along the passage.

— Did you find my note?

— You look very happy.

— I am very happy, says Madeleine, I've got wonderful news.

— I know you have, I say.

— Oh?

She looks at me. She's out of breath – running or something – and with all those bags – shopping – spending money – there's something reckless going on.

— I spoke to Nicholas.

— Nicky? How is Nicky?

— He's thrilled, I say.

— What about?

— Everything. Everything thrills him. Everything is thrilling. Nicholas is perpetually thrilled.

— Don't make fun of the poor boy. It's his job to be positive.

— The house needs painting.

— Does it?

— Of course it does.

But she's unstoppable. If the house needs painting, she'll see to it, she'll be up there on a ladder if necessary. She even smiles as she says:

— Have you been drinking?

— I had lunch, if that's what you mean.

— What? With Nicky? Did he say anything to you?

— Alone, actually.

— But you spoke to him?

— He wants me to take a sabbatical.

— That's weird. What kind of sabbatical?

— Why did you tell him about the telly thing?

— Oh? Did he mention that?

So innocent. So bright. What next? She's rummaging in the bags.

— Yes he did mention that, I say.

— I just wanted to make it sound like you were doing something. I was trying to support you. I'm sorry.

— I am doing something.

— I know you are.

— I am doing something. But not that. You had no right to talk about it.

— In which case forgive me.

Suddenly she hoists herself up on to the edge of the table and sits there swinging her legs like a child. Her eyes 'sparkle' as she bites her lip in pure and shameless pleasure.

— You left the TV on again.

— Don't be so boring, says Madeleine.

She straightens her legs and points her toes. She wants me to notice the new shoes. She waggles her feet.

— Don't be so boring, she says.

— What d'you expect me to do?

— I expect you to kiss me.

— What if I don't want to kiss you?

— You have no choice, says Madeleine, you're my husband.

It sounds obscene, as if she'd just said: 'You're my cunt.' The shoes are like birds – or the beaks of birds. She makes them dart and peck. She can't take her eyes off them.

— Is that why you lied to me?

— Lied to you? I don't understand.

— Because I'm your husband?

— How did I lie to you?

— About the play.

34

— How did I lie to you about the play? What play?

— You know what play, Madeleine.

— I didn't 'lie'. I don't know what you're talking about. What d'you think of my shoes? Aren't they nice?

— You'd already been offered the part. You'd already accepted the part. You didn't tell me. You lied to me.

— That's a very strange definition of a lie – but the fact is, is I only got the phone call after you went out to your meeting or whatever it was.

— And you accepted?

— Well of course I accepted.

— You're not going to do this play, Madeleine.

— I beg your pardon?

— I said you're not going to do this play.

She stops waggling the shoes. She looks up from her feet. Her face has changed: the false girlishness gone out of it.

— What? she says.

— You heard what I said, Madeleine. You don't need to look at me like that. That girl is completely mad.

— What girl? I'm lost.

— The writer.

— So? Is she? What if she is? What's it to you?

— She talks about being buried alive.

— What if she does? Maybe that's how she feels. Maybe that's how lots of us feel.

— Us?

— Women.

Please God – not this again.

— I don't want you to get involved, that's all.

— Involved? It's a play, John, not a relationship.

— A play *is* a relationship, Madeleine, as you well know. And this is a bad one. Believe me. I'm just trying to be honest with you.

— Well that's extremely kind, but I'd rather you were honest with yourself.

— Meaning what exactly?

35

When did she acquire this ability to make my skull feel transparent? It's as if years of scrutiny have worn away the bone. Whatever happened to the privacy of my thoughts? She's always there, looking in, like a warder at the peephole. The bird flaps round my head. Its steel beak scrapes against the door and sparks fly. The eye sees everything.

— Meaning what, Madeleine?

— Meaning you're jealous. Of me and of her. Meaning you don't want me to succeed. Or anyone to succeed. You're so full of hate. Why are you so full of hate?

— This part is degrading, Madeleine. It's sick and degrading. The simple truth is he's offered it to you because no other actress in their right mind would go near it – because he knows you're desperate. I am not full of hate. On the contrary: I'm saying this because I love you. I love you and I want you to stop making a fool of yourself.

— You love me?

— Is that funny?

— It's certainly unexpected, says Madeleine. It's certainly a long time since I've had any material evidence.

She retains that cynical, suggestive grin for another second or two before performing the most extraordinary movement: her face jerks away to the side and she begins to slide back from me along the top of the table, as if being pulled suddenly by a rope. The first things to go are the dirty mugs, cracking apart on the floor. The sugar spills and the dregs from the smashed glasses bleed into it. The knife flicks up out of the jam. The jam pot rolls. The knife lands and begins to spin. There goes the teapot: it splits open along its glazed surface – tea seeps out of the mass of wet leaves. There goes the empty milk bottle, and the bottle next to it with milk still in it. There go the teaspoons, the car keys, the door keys, the crumbs, the burnt crusts. There go the bills and the reminders for the bills and their envelopes with windows through which we could see our own names.

The candlesticks from Daddy jump off the table. The candles fracture but the thread inside holds the broken parts together. The stems snap off yesterday's wine glasses and the bowls of the glasses break into shards like tulip petals. The pepperpot explodes. And all this with the most terrible clatter and ringing while Madeleine slides back and back losing one shoe after the other – one on the floor – one on the table – or glides perhaps would be the better word – glides as if pulled by a rope wound into a machine – before she rolls off the edge – one hand up to her face – the other out to break her fall – flailing – trying to grip, trying to stop – on to the pile of newspapers. Then almost immediately she's back on her feet, 'finding her feet' almost immediately like an overturned cat, that hand still clutched to her face, covering her eye. She's running out of the room. She's running up the stairs. A door slams. Well!

I don't think my mum and dad ever came back to the house. They didn't like the house. It was too tall. If they stood on the front steps and looked up at it they felt as if they were falling backwards. If they looked out of the upstairs windows, they could see too far, they could see the whole city, which was also something that could make you dizzy. They didn't like what happened in the house even though they had no idea what happened in the house, only an impression: a cheeky young girl flicking her ash into a 'crystal' vase. They were 'quick to judge' – (meaning my mum, because my dad, of course, never let you know what he was thinking) – and that's why they never came back. They were offered tickets to see Madeleine, but they said no they were busy, it was too far. Or they said yes, they'd love to, and the tickets were posted to them – but on the night there'd be two empty adjacent seats in the middle of the stalls. And at those performances my mum and dad were far more present than if they'd bothered to turn up. The two empty seats on those nights had an alert and destructive life of their own. When everyone around them burst into applause, they quite deliberately sat with their arms folded, poisoning the celebration.

I pushed the door. It gave a little, in a spongy kind of way, but it didn't open. I knew exactly what she was doing: she was sitting on our bedroom floor with her back against the door. I might've pushed harder. I could push harder and force my way in, but then what? I was concerned for her, but she'd very cleverly set up the scene so that if I proved my concern by forcing my way in, the use of force would not only cancel out my concern but provide further evidence of what she would inevitably call my 'brutality'.

— Madeleine? Let me in. Are you alright?

I could hear that she was crying.

— Is your eye alright? Would you like me to get a flannel? D'you want me to look at it?

I waited a little – I knew this game, oh yes – and tried the door again. It began to swing freely, then banged shut in my face: she must've shoved hard back against it.

— Madeleine.

— Go away.

— I'm sorry.

— Go away.

She'd been right about the house: you couldn't breathe here, let alone work or think. She knew that, but she'd agreed to it anyway. I'd never understood that change of heart next to the stream. Perhaps it was just one more symptom of her perversity. Because the house shut out the world and once the world was shut out, what was left? Simply this squalid argument between husband and wife on either side of a closed door.

Still, I wanted to go into the room. I wanted to be forgiven. She owed me that much: forgiveness. But more than that, I wanted to be told there was nothing to forgive. I wanted her to see – to admit – because in the end she would have to admit – to the enormity of her provocation. I wanted to play back to her the look on her face. I wanted her to hear the cynical intonation of her own words.

I tried the door one more time, but now it was completely rigid. I realised she'd stretched her legs out in front of her so as to tense them like rods against the side of the big wardrobe. If the crying had stopped it was because she was concentrating on turning her body into a machine.

— Madeleine?

No answer.

I wrap up the shoes (each shoe has its own soft bag) and put them back into the shoe-box. I get down on my hands and knees, pick up the big pieces and sweep up the rest. I rescue the bills: the bills have survived. But the play is covered in jam and fragments of glass, and is beyond saving.

Stage Kiss

What kind of actor? Well let's just say you'd almost certainly know my face, but might not know my name. One
evening, for example, on the way home from a performance (I'm walking back to my flat), a young man stops me.
He's wearing the kind of hat whose earflaps fasten at the
crown. He blocks the path. 'I don't know your name,' he
says, 'but I saw the show and I've been thinking about it.
Tell me, he says, that moment, that moment when you kiss
the girl, is your tongue in her mouth? And what about hers?
What does she do with hers?'

I like streets. I like the slight unevenness of the paving
stones, the map-shapes on the trunks of plane trees. I enjoy
the movement of traffic, the separation of lanes, the use
of indicator lamps. At night, why is it that looked at in
a certain way buildings take on the aspect of ruins? The
lintels of the doorways, the laborious pointing of the
bricks, become mysteries whose function can no longer be
explained. Occasionally on my walks I pass a street lamp
buzzing violently behind its slim galvanised door. Some of
these galvanised doors have been smashed in – wires dangle
in the cavity – but the lamp is still shining. What strange
gleam of metal light on the green fingers of chestnut leaves!

From time to time after the show I meet up with our
director. The two of us go to a kind of café or club I suppose you'd call it, popular with people in the business –
the Safety Curtain. This club (cosy despite the terrible
name) has mirrors along the walls. One night our director
looks into the mirror beside him. He starts to make faces
and pull at his skin. It's quite alarming the way he's pulling
the loose skin of his cheeks right down. 'Fuck,' he says.
'Fuck. Is that what I look like? Is that really what I look

like?' I have to laugh. He's raised his voice. It's a little embarrassing.

Outside the theatre signs hang by chains from the canopy. They say things like this:

MAGNIFICENT

or:

HUGELY ENTERTAINING

We've collected a whole row of them and they remind me of railway stations or hospitals. Like the queue for returns, they continue round the side of the building. As you make your way to the stage door you pass beneath one which says:

TWO SUBTLY EROTIC PERFORMANCES

I know he's in love with Clair, but this is embarrassing. I say to him: 'Keep your voice down. *You* don't need reassuring. It's *us*, the actors, who are the vulnerable ones.' Vulnerable. He doesn't believe that for a moment. He's not prepared to be deceived, and that makes him intolerable. I want nothing to do with this, and I tell him so.

These feelings are at their most destructive when they interfere with the work. For example, he always refused – although of course in a roundabout way – to rehearse the kiss. And when we did finally pin him down, all he would say was: 'Go for it.' We're standing in the middle of the rehearsal room, talking very quietly, intimately, his arms around us. Clair catches my eye. She finds this physical contact repellent, that's obvious. She's biting her lip, trying not to laugh. He can't see that. He's bowed his head between us. It's hanging there. For a moment it's as if he's lifeless and we're holding up a corpse. The kiss? He raises his head and smiles. 'Better just go for it, boys and girls.'

Tomorrow I'm visiting Steph, my dentist. She's gradually replacing the black fillings in my molars with tooth-coloured material. I love these visits. It's so silent out here, in the suburbs, where Steph lives. Even though there's plenty of space outside, I park my car (it's surprisingly modest) a few streets away just for the pleasure of walking past houses which, although similar, have all been treated differently by their owners. Some have planted a screen of fast-growing conifers. Others have stripped the paint off their front doors. One house has a 'hand-made' ceramic number plate, with a pattern of entwined flowers. Another has its three digits – 149 – stuck to the front gate with self-adhesive stickers. The numerals are black-on-silver and slant like italics. Not so long ago I would have held all this in contempt – curtains chosen to match wallpaper, the life-like statuette of a cat about to pounce from the garage roof, the half-barrel planted with an azalea – but now (I'm nearly fifty but I don't look it), particularly when the light is low and rakes across the lawns and flowerbeds, I find in these things a quite extraordinary beauty. Some of the wooden gateposts have little plaques announcing professions, e.g. 'Teacher of Pianoforte', 'Chiropodist'. Unlike the polished brass plates you find in a city, these are made of hard black plastic with letters in white or grey. Stephanie's is no exception, and lists her qualifications. The Victorian bays of the front elevation are filled with white Venetian blinds. However, this is deceptive, the treatment room itself being on the ground floor at the back of the house. Through French windows framed by rust-coloured vine leaves the client is treated to a view of Stephanie's back garden. She injects at the base of the tooth, and the needle grates against the buried root. These days she wears surgical gloves for all procedures.

Back at the stage door, Colin hands me a copy of the London *Evening Standard*. Picture of you, he says. In fact, it's a picture of me and Clair. We're holding hands at an HIV charity dinner. We both look tremendously famous and happy. The flashlight has detached us from the background, making us look startlingly attractive, capable of anything. We are the embodiment of the word 'abandon' or the phrase 'throw caution to the wind'. My free hand is plucking streamers from my DJ. Clair, similarly draped, is wearing a short stretch dress, and the arbitrary moment of the picture has caught her legs at an odd angle, as if she's suffered a spinal injury. But did I say smile? No, our mouths are both wide open. We're positively howling with laughter. Look at us. We're like two rare nocturnal animals whose antics have triggered a tripwire in a remote clearing.

Some actors are jokers and I'm afraid I'm one of them. Not just offstage (locking fellow actors in their dressing rooms when they're called, telling Colin that I can smell smoke and making him summon a fire-engine to the Wednesday matinée) but also onstage. At critical moments I'm very fond of whispering comic remarks to the person I'm acting with. Alternatively I play the fool in the wings, the aim being to distract somebody else's scene. This is perfectly innocent behaviour, and some of the actors find it enormously funny, but there are one or two (you always get one or two) who will no longer speak to me.

After the show I may go to the Safety Curtain, or on to a party, but usually I just walk home. I say that people know my face, but the mere act of walking generally protects me from recognition. In Charing Cross Road for example, I become invisible. This enables me to unwind in the video arcades where I go not as a player, but as a spectator. Our play is a costume piece and the machines are a refreshing reminder of the twentieth century. Some of them simulate driving racing cars or flying a plane – to complete the illusion you climb right into them. After the initial impression of chaos you're finally overwhelmed here by a sense of order: patterns of light, which appear random, start to repeat themselves, needle-like blips of sound gradually become recognisable as fragments of Mozart, Beethoven etc.

Once I take my turning I'm virtually there. It's a small street, really a lane, the pavement lined with bollards. I rarely see anyone in this lane, but two incidents stay in my mind. In the first, a young woman with fair hair and a black dress is running towards me. She ducks into a doorway where she changes into a different pair of shoes. She then runs on. In the second, I find myself walking behind a young couple with arms around each other, male and female. The man pulls his free hand out of his trouser pocket, and as he does so a key drops to the ground. I run after them with the key. Oh, says the man, I don't need that any more. They then walk on.

A plastic card and PIN number give me access to a lobby with exquisitely maintained plants. A private lift takes me directly into my apartment. No one comes here. I sleep deeply. I don't dream.

Most Sundays I visit my wife. I say 'my wife' although – notoriously – we are divorced. I drive down to the coast (my car is surprisingly modest) and if the weather is fine we'll spend the afternoon in the garden (we both hate the sea) until dark. I often cut the grass with an old hand-mower, feeling thoroughly domestic, before sitting back at the slatted patio table to watch the alternate bands of light and dark with their exaggerated perspective. When I've done this it becomes a true seaside garden, bringing to mind miniature golf, speedboat rides, red-and-white lighthouses, the brittle crust of toffee-apples. My wife reminds me that I once said to her: 'Have you noticed how men leave their wives when they become famous? I'm just waiting to become famous.' She says this without rancour, as if describing the shape of an afternoon cloud, or the habits of the songbirds she feeds with bacon fat. She's interested in Stephanie, and asks to look at my teeth. Having done so, she says: It's strange – you seem to have spent your life growing younger.

Only when it's completely dark do we go indoors. I've been asked to free a jammed cassette. The Sunday supplements seem to like the fact that I began life as a stage manager, and it's quite true that I have a gift for this kind of work. There's a green felt noticeboard in the kitchen

45

with the usual papers pinned all over it – this month's calendar (it's October), coupons for money-off toothpaste, handy phone numbers (plumber, pizzas, minicab), and among all these I notice that someone – presumably one of the children – has pinned up the photo from the *Standard*. It seems to have been assigned no particular prominence: indeed, the picture is already half-covered with a final demand for the telephone.

It doesn't take long to extract the cassette: Schubert's Piano Sonata in B Flat played on a Viennese piano of 1828, the year of his death. By the time I've unearthed the solvent and thoroughly cleaned the heads and pinch-roller with a cotton bud, it's time to go.

From the front garden the sea is audible. My car stands just outside the gate, in the moonlight. The last thing my wife says to me is, 'Are you happy?' to which I reply, 'Are you?' In the theatre, these lines could prove unplayable, and I'd suggest a cut.

The moment of the kiss is violent, technical, prolonged. Clair's character initiates it. I'm playing the kind of part I often seem to be offered nowadays: the older man – solitary, apparently cold – but with an undercurrent of re-pressed sensuality. And as Clair – or Clair's character – pulls me down on to the chaise, we must avoid (a) letting the stalls see all the way up her dress (slippery green satin) and (b) crushing her (I've recently started to put on weight). At the same time, as I've said, it must be forceful and aban-doned, and I think we've started to achieve that. By push-ing one of my knees up between her legs as I fall, we solve the weight-bearing and sight-line problems simultane-ously, as well as making it quite clear that sexual inter-course will follow. Even without direction, the kiss at its best can still contain the truth of all the kisses I've known: the kisses of the girl who became 'my wife' and lives by the sea, the frightening kisses which came outside my marriage and – notoriously – destroyed it, other kisses on stage, kisses on film. How can I regret any of these when each contributes to the work and feeds the intensity of this one stage kiss which night after night shocks a packed house into what the critics quite rightly describe as rapture?

Sometimes, though, just before our lips touch, I'm afraid I can't resist whispering one of my little comments, the joy being Clair's extreme susceptibility. Just the movement of an eyebrow is often enough to set her off. As I go down I push my knee into the usual place, but from the way her fingertips dig into me I can tell she's lost all control. This is why she's so desperate for my mouth to cover hers. It's a scream. Her back arches. She's choking. We kiss.

In the auditorium: silence, rapture, the same, exactly the same. No inkling of deceit.

WRITING FOR THEATRE

Party

Party was first performed on 23 June 2010 as part of the Royal Court's post-election *Hung-Over* event at Theatre Local, Unit 215, Elephant and Castle Shopping Centre, London. The cast included:

Annette Badland, Claudie Blakley, Stephen Boxer, Charles Mnene, Sophie Okonedo, Ukweli Roach, Martin Savage, Angela Terence

Directed by Simon Godwin

—   I feel great.

—   I'm feeling good.

—   At last!

—   At last!

—   Yes at last someone's making a decision. At last a rich person is making a decision.

—   At long last a poor person's fate is decided by the rich. It's great.

—   It's great – I'm really pleased.

—   It's great to be rich *plus* really good to be poor if a rich person's in control.

—   It's a great time to be poor. It's a great time to have nothing.

—   Really good for the market.

—   *Great* for the markets: *great* to be really poor.

—   Everyone wins.

—   Great to be rich. Really good to be rich. Great evening to have the top down on your luxury car – great day for bankers!

—   Everyone wins: even the whites, even the blacks win. Even the sexy tots look happy!

—   Oh happy tots! Oh happy Ministers of State for Culture and Rape!

—— Oh beaming Minister for Love My God.

—— I just love my God.

—— Yes so do I! I *really* love my God – in fact my God *is* love.

—— Well hey – so 's mine.

—— Mine too.

—— That's weird.

—— That's fucking weird.

—— That's weird but look – look – look – I really respect your religion.

—— Yes and I respect yours too.

—— I really respect everyone's religion and especially when it involves a sex-crime – there's something about that kind of crime that makes good feelings resonate throughout the world.

—— Do what?

—— Resonate.

—— Resonate throughout the world.

—— I want to be there. I want to hold the knife. I want to smear the blood. I want to mix the cum with the blood.

—— Well let me say this to you: you can!

—— I can?

—— You can – yes you can – the knife is yours – and so is the tender victim. Everyone wins.

—— Even the victim wins: it's that kind of party – it's the kind of party where even the victim wins.

—— Okay: so when does it start?

56

—— When does it start? When does it start? It's started. It's real. It's now. It's happening. It's cuddly *plus* it's violent.

—— You mean like a cat?

—— I mean like a cat or I mean like a violent teddy-bear.

—— You mean like a violent teddy-bear?

—— Yes that is exactly what I mean: I mean like a teddy-bear when you wake up in the night and you find that your teddy has spattered your face with acid. I mean like that.

—— Sounds great!

—— Sounds really great!

—— Yes and when you try to crawl to the bathroom sink you find that your violent teddy or your violent cat – guess what! – has taped your legs to the bed.

—— Oh no!

—— Yes taped up your legs and your face just burns and burns and burns *plus* you're now blind.

—— Oh no! It sounds hilarious!

—— It's really really great – but hey! it's that kind of party – it's the kind of party where everyone's welcome – where the religious observances of white men have been carefully considered and the dietary requirements of white men have been carefully considered and the accessibility issues of able-bodied white men have been very very carefully considered and so have the special needs of each white man's penis *plus* all women regardless of race *or* body-mass will be given the

57

human right to choose whichever hospital they think will best cosmetically restructure their vagina.

—— Really good for the market.

—— *Great* for the markets – really great news for bankers *and* for the genitals of bankers' wives.

—— Great news for teddy-bears.

—— Great great news for sexy tots and for people who have nothing: oh the games they can now play! – the game of *Murder for Oil* – the game of *Murder for Growth*.

—— The game of *Murder in Palestine*.

—— The *Let's Blindfold and Murder the Demented, Shall We* game.

—— The hilarious party-game of *Assist the Disabled to Go to Switzerland and Pay to Be Killed* – all currencies accepted.

—— All languages spoken – except, naturally, Greek – and yes! yes! yes! this is the party where all currencies are accepted and anyone can pick up a scalpel right now and operate –

—— Conjoined twins!

—— Can – yes – not separate, but make right now conjoined twins!

—— – where each human being – and this is new – has the human right (you're right) right now to be surgically joined to another's hip or to another's shit-filled bowel – where we can join right now right here at the party the brain of the screaming columnist to the brain of the abusive priest – where using a monkey's spine we can cleverly connect the neck of the Minister for

Torture and the Arts to the TV commentator's
arsehole not just for the duration of this party
but for life – connect the two of them for life.
But hey! – it's messy – watch out for the blood!

—— Attention: slippery floor!

—— Slippery floor – watch out for the bits of jelly.

—— Watch out for the bits of bone, yes, and jelly.

—— Watch out for the slippery cum and the slippery
chocolate.

—— Watch out.

—— Watch out.

—— Watch out for the beer and spit.

—— Watch out for the dance-floor fuckers and the
fuckers fucking in the toilet.

—— Watch out for the white girls in the pink limo –
watch out for those black boys in the bright-blue
ties. Mind they don't slip!

—— Mind no one slips on the slippery floor during
the hilarious games. Take care!

—— Take care.

—— Take care.

—— Yes please take very special care not to damage
the poor: you will need them to clear up. You
will need them to take drugs and murder their
babies.
   But listen: great party.

—— Thank you.

—— Great party.

—— Thank you.

—— Great party.

—— Thank you. Thank you.

In the Valley

In the Valley was first performed at the Royal Court
Theatre Upstairs as part of its *Surprise Theatre* season
on 16 July 2013.

Performed by Michael Gould

Directed by Katie Mitchell

Well.

Here I am.

I've made it: I've survived. I speak. I move. It's great. It's great to speak.

I'm not sympathetic.

Let's get that out of the way: let's put it on the table in front of us – like the car-keys. *Not sympathetic.*

But look: what car-keys? What table? Good question.

I want to thank you.

I want to thank you for this opportunity.

I want to thank you.

I speak, I move, it's great, it might not've been so great, but it is, it's really great.

The light is great here.

It's really good light.

But there is a problem – not with the light – there's no problem with the light – but there is a problem all the same.

Oh dear my little boy died of cancer. Not true. Oh dear there's been a terrible accident. Not true. Oh dear a horrid attack by terrorists. Not true, not true. Great light. Really good. Oh no: that little girl was raped. No – not true. Not about that. It's not about that. That's not the problem. What problem? I'll come to that later.

I'm here. I've made it. I speak, I move – but very little. I've noticed how little I move. I could be sympathetic but

I'm not. It could be about the poor but it's not. I could be poor but oh dearie me I'm not. But at least I'm here.

I'm here and I've survived. It's a long way. It's a long walk. I made it. I tripped. I fell. I got to my feet. I smiled. Correction: tried to smile. I got to my feet, I tried to smile. There was a valley. I entered it. I crossed the valley floor. There was a spring. I drank from it. Drank from the spring? I think not. No. *Drank from the spring?* No.

I heard the news. What news? The new news. I clicked on the news. I listened to the newest news. I watched the news. There was the news: I watched it. The news was great. It was great great news. I tried to smile. I thought of my friend. I clicked on my friend. I looked at my friend. I closed my friend. I closed the news. I clicked on my mind: my mind opened. I closed it again.

The valley's great, the valley's green. What's that at the end of the valley? Oh that's a sheep. A sheep, that's great, that's good, it's good to see a sheep like that in a valley, grazing, I love it. A long walk, a long long walk, then suddenly: the sheep. Quick! Take a photograph! Well no. Obviously not. No battery, no camera.

Me and the sheep we get on really well. Can you believe that? I can hardly believe it myself – but it's true. The sheep has fine taste in literature and music but is afraid of foxes. Whatever we discuss – Cervantes – the keyboard works of William Byrd – sooner or later the sheep comes back to foxes – 'Can you smell fox?' – 'Look at this fox-bite' – it's fox fox fox all day long. 'There can't be much to do,' I say to the sheep, 'in this valley of yours. You must miss civilisation, and culture.' 'Hmm,' says the sheep, 'not sure what you mean – you'll need to define your terms.' The sheep leads me to the spring. The water is seeping up, making a clear pool in

the grass. Oh how the water magnifies the green blades!
'This is the spring,' says the sheep, 'and you're welcome
to drink – but remember: it's just when your head's down
to drink and you're enjoying the cold spring water – it's
just then you're most vulnerable to foxes.' Yes, me and
the sheep could get on really well, if it wasn't for this
fox obsession. I'd like to say can we please please leave
foxes out of it, at least for a few hours – but how can I
say that? – the sheep is my host – (I can't believe I'm
really saying that, saying *the sheep is my host*) – I can't
offend it – it could turn nasty. I mean have you looked at
its teeth? have you seen the way it stares when it thinks
you won't notice?

It's not about the poor but I want to reassure you about
the poor. The poor people are doing fine. Yes. You don't
have to worry. They've got shoes. They've got some
quite nice jeans. They're doing fine. Click on the poor
and you'll see they've got their own street – not bad,
having your own street. If you want to buy a used toy
rabbit or a cooking ladle, this is the place to come. There's
a man here wears a silver cowboy-hat. Quick: close him.

*

I have seen God.
Let's get that out of the way too.
Because ha ha ha, you are thinking – not true.
But it is a fact that I've seen God. I've seen him in my
kitchen. And I've see him in my entrance hall.
Back in the day: back in the day, I mean, of kitchens and
of entrance halls – before the valley, before the sheep.

Yes the light here is great – I've said it: great great light –
but the light *then* – the light in my kitchen *then* – oh –
miraculous! And the way God crawled – yes the way
God crawled under my kitchen table to escape the
miraculous light and whimpered as if he was ashamed!

Come out, I said, come out – and poked him with a stick.

Since God was a him alright!
There was the old man's arse, and there – look – were the white-haired balls since God – fact – God was naked.
Yes there were the white-haired balls – but where was his face?
I wanted him to turn.
I wanted to see God's face.
But there was a bag, and the bag stayed over his head.
Ha ha ha, you are thinking – ha ha ha – not true. But the plastic bag stayed – yes it did – at all times over his head.

Oh the way God whimpered!
Oh the way the bag shrank when he inhaled and puffed up when he breathed out again!
Oh, how the white bag crackled!

Had he been at the rubbish?
Had he poked his head into the bag the way a fox might to get at some scrapings, then found he was stuck?
And why – yes why were God's hands tied behind his back like that with a plastic cable-tie?
I refused to speculate.
I prodded his arse.
I loved him.

Oh how I loved my God! And oh how the same breath that animated – correction – tried to animate – that tried to animate the universe now puffed up then sucked back in the crackling bag!
This was one in the eye for the sceptics. This was one in the eye for the unpickers – and how I hated them! – of human thread.

Yes how I detested the unpickers of human thread
poking their needles into the human fabric so that the
human fabric came apart – who'd stripped human beings
of their thread the way that looters in a war zone strip
buildings of their copper wire to sell the copper.
I'd seen them unravel the world.
I'd watched them – oh yes watched them back in the day
winding the world's thread into their own profitable
machines – heard them adopt a tone – listened to them
sneer plus listened to them ridicule in best-selling
paperbacks the idea even of a created world.

But of course you'll be wondering – sorry – why I had
a stick.
I had a stick because I'd been planting out my sweet-peas.
I had a stick because when summer came the pale pink
and the pale blue flowers were going to bloom on a
black frame of sticks like this one in my hand.

I had a stick because their strong scent was going to
perfume one hot corner of my garden until green pods
appeared at the heart of the dead petals and grew and
grew and filled with next year's seeds.
I had a stick – but who cares why I had a stick!
I had a stick – fact.
I prodded God's arse with it – fact.
I said to God come out. I said to God don't whimper.
I wanted to pull off the bag and see God's face.
I wanted to know who'd tortured him.
I loved my God but who had tortured him?
Who'd tied up his hands like that and left him naked?
Who'd bruised his arse?
Who'd hung him from a beam till his arms at some point
split out of his shoulders?
Was it the angels?

Why were the angels angry?
Why did the angels so suddenly scent blood?
What did they blame him for?
Their own stupidity?
Or was it they blamed him for the whole human disaster?
But what did they expect?
Didn't they know how hard it was to animate the world?
Didn't they know how much concentration it took to
open just one pink flower?
Hadn't I had my own plastic cow and got my own
plastic milkmaid down on the plastic stool to milk her?
Hadn't I had my own metal circus and a doll I could
make cry?
I'd got the farmer to talk to the chicken and the cat to
have a conversation with the duck.
I married the fairy to the beast, forced the pirates to
surrender plus re-attached their victims' heads.
I'd built whole cities in an afternoon, injected the
inhabitants and fed them slices of banana. I knew how
hard it was.
And if it had been hard to keep my plastic water-skier
for example in her blue bikini attached for just five
minutes to James Bond 007's plastic speedboat, then
how much more difficult it must be to breathe life as
God must eternally – and here he was! – into an
expanding universe.

God would not turn.
However hard I prodded him God would not turn.
God would not speak.
I said: God would not speak.
God would not say he loved me.

*

It's not nice to admit, but I'm afraid I began to eat the
sheep. What choice did I have? – I'm human. Yes I am
human. I tried not to harm it. I sliced off small pieces
at a time and roasted them. I had no choice. I had no
choice if I wanted to survive and speak. Each time I cut
the sheep it screamed. Necessary – but still pretty horrid.
I promised it a trip to the Rijksmuseum to see the
Rembrandts, which it only knew from reproductions.
What was I supposed to do? – eat grass?

Don't look at me like that. I took care. I bound the
wound. I washed the rag each morning at the spring and
reapplied it. I cleaned the knife. I kept the blade sharp.
I said don't look at me like that: I kept the blade sharp –
I tried to avoid the bone.

*

It was on about the thirtieth day – as I was leaving the
valley – after stripping the sheep of meat – that the man
with the silver cowboy-hat entered my mind. Yes.

Of course I had feared this. I had always feared the man
with the silver cowboy-hat. Now here he was, standing
quietly in the corner, with his face turned away. 'How
did you get into my mind?' I said. 'I selected it,' said the
man with the silver cowboy-hat, 'and clicked. Don't
worry. I'm just going to stand here. I don't take up much
room. Soon you won't even notice me.'

And ha ha ha you're thinking – he's telling me what to
say. But no. Oh no. Not true. It's me. It's me that speaks.
It's me that moves. It's me that thanks you for this
opportunity. It's me that says, 'I'll come to the problem
later.' Me who survived. Me who listened to the newest
news. Who tripped – who fell – who got to his feet –
who smiled. It's me who entered the valley, befriended
the sheep and ate it. Me who saw reflected in the blade
of the knife the grey gleam of the sky!

But all the same. Yes all the same he does sometimes ask
me questions.

'Where are the car-keys?' he might say – or 'What
happened to your kitchen table?' 'Whose breath exactly' –
he'll ask me – 'filled the crackling bag?' 'Are you quite
sure you're alive?' he sometimes says – 'and if so, what's
making you live?'

The Iron Rice Bowl

The Iron Rice Bowl was first performed at the Royal Court Theatre Downstairs on 12 June 2011 as part of an event for Human Rights Watch. The cast included:

Khalid Abdalla, Tunji Lucas, Helen McCrory, Sophie Okonedo

Directed by Simon Godwin

Characters

F1, F2, F3
female

M1, M2, M3
male

M1   A man comes into a room –

F1   Okay –

M1   He caresses a bowl –

F1   Oh?

M1   Yes – caresses an iron bowl –

F1   I see – a man –

M1   Yes.

F1   Does it have to be a man?

M1   What?

F1   I said: why does it always have to be a man?

      Pause.

M1   Well. Fine. Over to you.

F1   Thank you.

M1   Over to you – bitch.

F1   I'll ignore that.

F3   Did you just call her a bitch?

M1   Sure. Yes. Bitch. Yes. Over to you.

      Pause.

      I said over to you.

F1   A woman comes into a room –

M1   Okay.

M2	Great.
F1	Thank you. She caresses an iron bowl –
M2	Great. But try it with Coke.
F1	Caresses a Coke?
F3	Comes in with a Coke – yes?
F1	Great.
M2	Coke before bowl.
F1	Great.
M2	Happy?
F1	Sure. (*Slight pause.*) A woman comes into a room with a glass of Coke and caresses an iron bowl.
F3	The weather?
F1	Is warm.
F3	The room?
F1	Is well-lit.
F3	The Coke?
F2	Nice and cold. There's ice.
M2	Great.
F2	Plus lemon.
M2	Great. Happy?
F1	Sure. Of course she is. She's got the Coke, she's got the bowl. She's got the good vibe in the well-lit room. Sure. Great. Over to you.
M1	To me?
F1	Why not? – Pig.
M1	Don't call me a pig.

M2   You called her bitch.

M1   But she ignored it.

F3   Hey!

M1   What?

F3   Concentrate.

      Pause.

M1   Sure.

F1   Over to you.

M1   Sure.

M2   Happy?

M1   Sure.

F3   Coke before bowl – yes?

M1   Got it.

F3   Great.

M1   Okay. (*Slight pause.*) A woman comes into a
      room. She's holding a glass of Coke. It's warm
      in the well-lit room. She caresses an iron bowl,
      then pings the rim. Smiles – says – 'Count me
      out. Hundreds dead – so what? Child skidding
      on blood – so what?' Says – 'Help who, why?'
      Says – 'Help who how for what?' – or – better –
      'Change what for who where when, bitch?
      Hands off my bowl.'

F2   (*slight pause*) Great.

M1   Then dims the light.

F2   Great. Thank you. Question.

F1   Oh?

M1   Sure.

F2   Question about the ping.

M1   Say it.

F2   How does the rim ping?

M1   How does the rim ping? Short.

F1   Short?

M1   Yes it's a short ping – happy?

F2   And the dim?

M1   What about it?

F2   Is the dim –?

M2   Good question.

F2   – thank you – is the dim short too? Well?

       Pause.

M1   Let's say it's a long dim.

F3   Great. Contrast. Love it. (*Points at M3.*) Happy?

M3   Me?

F3   Are you?

M3   Me? Sure.

F3   Great. Just that you've not yet spoken.

M3   Me?

F3   No. Why? Why have you not yet spoken? Why aren't you taking part?

F2   Hey!

F3   What? What? Nobody just says nothing. Or is this a protest? Are you protesting? Well? And if so about what?

F2   Hey!

M3   No.

F3   So you're not.

M3   No.

F3   Then contribute.

M3   Sure. (*Takes time to think, then:*) Let's say . . .
      why don't we say . . . that this metal bowl . . .
      is a crucible of fire.

      Pause. The others all stare at M3.

F1   Love it.

M2   Happy?

M3   Sure.

M2   Happy?

M3   Sure.

M2   Happy?

F1   (*to M2*) Just stop being a dick.

M1   Don't call him a dick.

F3   You called her bitch, pig.

F2   Hey!

M1   Well, that is my human right.

F2   Hey!

M1   That is my human right – friend.

F2   Great – but – please – stop.

F3   Pig.

F2   Please.

M1   Sure.

F2   Let's wrap this up now.

M2   Great.

M1   Sure.

F2   Please?

       Pause.

       Over to you.

F1   Me?

F2   Please. Happy?

F1   Sure.

F3   Short ping – yes?

F1   Got it.

F2   So.

       Pause.

F1   A woman comes into a well-lit room. She sips
       from a glass of Coke, caresses the iron bowl,
       then pings the rim. Short ping of rim, warm from
       a low flame. She smiles – says – 'Listen, count
       me out. Hundreds dead – so what? Child
       skidding on blood, man swinging on rope – so
       what?' Says – 'Help who, why?' Says – 'Change
       what for who where how? I'm safe in my bowl.'
       She turns up the flame, climbs into the iron bowl
       and screws shut the lid. Black in the bowl first.
       Then red heat. Short scream from within. Then
       white incandescence. (*Pause.*) Then after the
       flame ends – well – what? Long dim. Sing-song
       of the cooling metal.

Vaclav and Amelia

Vaclav and Amelia, a co-production by Théâtre Garonne de Toulouse and Zoé & Cie, was first performed in a double bill with Harold Pinter's *Ashes to Ashes* on 5 May 2009 at Théâtre Garonne de Toulouse. The cast included:

Aurélia Alcaïs, Magne Havard Brakke, Jean-Marc Stehlé

Translated by Louis-Do de Lencquesaing
   and Gérard Watkins
Directed by Louis-Do de Lencquesaing
Costumes and Set Design by Jean-Marc Stehlé
Lighting by Gilles Gentner
Sound by Quentin Sirjacq

Characters

Amelia
late twenties

Vaclav
her husband

Farmer
an old man

Time
now

Place
remote farm

Interior farm building. Late afternoon. A table.
  Amelia alone.
  Vaclav enters.

Amelia Well?

Vaclav He's here.

Amelia Where?

Vaclav Outside.

Amelia What's he like?

Vaclav Seems kind.

Amelia Kind? (*Slight pause.*) And he understands you?

Vaclav Yes.

Amelia How do you know?

Vaclav How do I know? I've talked to him.

Amelia About what?

Vaclav About the journey. I've explained that you're
tired. I've explained that it's a very long journey and
that / you're tired.

Amelia I'm not tired. Why did you say that?

Vaclav You are tired, Amelia. In the taxi you were
falling asleep.

Amelia Taxi? It's a truck.

Vaclav Whatever.

Amelia That . . . thing is not a taxi, it's a truck. It's an animal truck.

Vaclav We won't argue, Amelia.

Amelia We won't argue, because it's a truck. (*Slight pause.*) Can't you just give him what he wants.

Vaclav You agreed to talk to him. That's why we're here.

Amelia's attention wanders, then:

Amelia What?

Vaclav That's why we're here.

Amelia I can see fields.

Vaclav I'm sorry?

Amelia When I shut my eyes.

Vaclav That's because you've been travelling.

Amelia What about you?

Vaclav If I shut my eyes?

Amelia Yes.

He shuts his eyes – concentrates.

Vaclav I see your face.

Amelia Don't.

Vaclav It's true.

She lets him take her head in his hands. Then:

Amelia Get him to come in.

Vaclav Mmm?

Amelia I said: get him to come in.

Vaclav goes out and returns with an old man, a Farmer. The Farmer wears a distinctive hat. He remains by the door.

Tell him to come closer. Why is he standing by the door like that? Tell him to come closer.

Vaclav Please. Come in. Come closer.

Farmer approaches the table, stares at Amelia.

Amelia Tell him to take off that hat. I don't want to see the hat. Take it off.

Slight pause.

Vaclav You can't ask / him to –

Amelia Tell him to take off his hat.

Vaclav Please – she would like you – if you don't mind it – to take off your hat.

Farmer takes off hat and steps forward to put it on the table.

Amelia Not on the table.

Vaclav What?

Amelia He's not to put his hat on the table. Tell him.

Farmer, however, has already got the idea, and remains clutching the hat.

He understands me.

Vaclav Of course he doesn't understand you.

Amelia (*to Farmer*) You understand me. Don't you.

Vaclav Of course he doesn't understand you.

Amelia Ask him. Ask him if he understands me.

Vaclav No.

Amelia Ask him.

Slight pause.

93

Vaclav She says: do you understand her?

Amelia What're you saying to him?

Vaclav I'm asking him.
　Do you understand what Amelia is saying?

Farmer I understand that she's travelled a long way and must be tired.

Amelia What did he say?

Vaclav He said no – of course he doesn't – of course he doesn't understand.

Amelia Then why is he smiling?

Vaclav He's not smiling.

Amelia Of course he's smiling. Look at him. Stop smiling. Why are you smiling?

　Slight pause.

Farmer (*smiles*) She's angry.

Amelia What did he say?

Vaclav He says you're angry.

Amelia Too fucking right I'm angry.

Farmer She's very angry.

Amelia Too fucking right. I don't like farms. I don't like farmers. And I don't like their hats. Tell him to put down his hat.

Vaclav Please. Put down your hat.

Amelia And not on the table.

Vaclav Not on the table. Perhaps – if you don't mind it – you could . . .

Amelia Why can't he just drop it? Tell him to just drop that disgusting hat / on the floor.

Vaclav Perhaps you could just put your hat on the floor.

Farmer stoops – with some difficulty, it seems – and puts his hat on the floor. Vaclav makes a move as if to help, but Amelia holds him back. Farmer straightens up again.

Thank you. May heaven bless. You must forgive us. For us this is all . . . um . . . (*Searches for word.*) unknown – no – strange.

Amelia What?

Vaclav I'm finding the word. I'm thanking him.

Amelia Tell him who you are.

Vaclav He knows who I am.

Amelia Tell him. Make it clear. I want to hear you make it clear to him.

Vaclav My name is Vaclav. I am this lady's husband. That's right – as I have said – we're married.

Amelia Are you telling him?

Vaclav Of course I'm telling him. I'm Vaclav and I am married to Amelia.

Amelia I don't belong here: make that clear.

Vaclav I love Amelia and Amelia is my wife.

Amelia Does he understand?

Vaclav Well of course he understands.

Amelia Ask him. Ask him if he understands.

Vaclav It's quite clear, Amelia, that he / understands.

Farmer Do you have children?

Vaclav (*slight pause*) No.

Amelia What did he say? (*Slight pause.*) What did he say?

Vaclav He's asking us if we have children.

Amelia Why're you asking us that?

Vaclav It's because I've told him that we're married.

Amelia No we don't. No we don't 'have any children'. Tell him.

Vaclav I've already told him.

Amelia Well tell him again. No we don't 'have any children'. (*Slight pause.*) Tell him. (*Slight pause.*) We don't want any children. Say it. (*Slight pause.*) I said: say it.

Vaclav We don't want any children.

Amelia In his language.

Vaclav We don't want any children. (*Slight pause.*) I would like to have children, but Amelia would not. (*Slight pause.*) I understand Amelia's . . . um . . . point of view, but I don't agree with it.

Amelia What're you saying to him?

Vaclav Mmm?

Amelia What're you saying to him? Why is he smiling like that?

Vaclav I'm explaining. I'm explaining that we don't want to have children.

Amelia You mean that I don't.

Vaclav Yes.

Amelia You mean that I don't want to have children.

Vaclav Yes.

Amelia Then why is he smiling?

Vaclav Because he understands, of course. Because he understands, and respects you.

Amelia Oh?

Vaclav Yes.

Amelia Respects me.

Vaclav Yes. (*Slight pause.*) Well yes: of course he does.

Farmer makes a sudden move, reaching into the pocket of his coat.

Amelia What's he doing? What's he getting out of his pocket? Stop him. I said: stop him.

Farmer suspends his gesture – looks up at her.

He stopped. He understands me. Don't you. You understand me. Don't you.

Pause. Amelia and Farmer stare at each other.

You see: he's not smiling now. (*Slight pause.*) Not smiling now, are you?

Vaclav Amelia . . .

Amelia Tell him he's stopped smiling.

Vaclav He knows he's stopped smiling.

Amelia Does he? Tell him.

Farmer It's fruit.

Amelia What?

Farmer I have fruit.

Vaclav He says it's fruit.

Amelia Says what's fruit?

97

Vaclav He means in his pocket – don't you – you have fruit in your pocket – yes?

Farmer Fruit. I have fruit from the tree.

Vaclav It's fruit – he says – from the tree.

Farmer gestures towards pocket:

Farmer Fruit from the tree.

They watch as the Farmer takes a bag out of his pocket. He puts the bag on the table and makes a gesture: 'accept this gift'.

Vaclav He wants you to open the bag.

Amelia He can open the bag himself. Tell him.

Vaclav Please. Open the bag.

Amelia Tell him.

Vaclav I've just told him.

Farmer I've picked this fruit from the tree.

Vaclav He's picked this fruit / from the tree.

Farmer Before daylight.

Vaclav What?

Farmer Before daylight. I picked it for your wife.

Vaclav He says it's for you.

Farmer It's for you.

Vaclav It's for you.

Amelia Then open it. If it's for me, open it.

Vaclav Please. Show us. Open it.

Farmer opens the bag and spills the fruit carefully on to the table. He takes back the bag and folds it up in a special way. The sight of the fruit softens Amelia's mood.

Amelia Thank you.

Vaclav Thank you. May heaven bless.

Amelia What marvellous fruit.

Vaclav What marvellous fruit.

Amelia No – honestly – it's really the most / marvellous fruit.

Vaclav No – honestly – it's really the most / marvellous fruit.

Amelia What is this fruit called?

Vaclav What is the name of this fruit?

Farmer Plums.

Amelia What?

Vaclav He says it's called plums.

Farmer Plums. (*Repeats 'accept this gift' gesture.*)

Vaclav The fruit is plums.

Amelia They're beautiful. Thank you.

She goes to the plums, picks one up and looks at it. She smiles.

They're still wet.

She lifts it to her face and savours the smell. She meets the Farmer's eyes. She bites into the plum.

Ah! (*Spits.*) Ah! (*Spits.*) Ah! it's disgusting!

As she continues to spit, the Farmer laughs.

Farmer The plums aren't to eat.

99

Vaclav They're not to eat.

Farmer You have to bottle them.

Vaclav Have to what?

Farmer You have to bottle the plums.

Vaclav You have to store – no – preserve – preserve the plums – is that right?

Farmer Bottle them.

Vaclav You have to preserve the plums – I think this is right – in bottles.

Farmer Work for women.

Vaclav What?

Farmer Work for women.

Vaclav Which is a job, he says, for women.

Amelia Well fuck that. Fuck his fucking jobs for women. Jesus Christ.

> *Still spitting out particles of fruit she turns and moves as far away as possible. Her back turned, she wipes her mouth with a tissue. Pause. Vaclav goes over to her, says her name, touches her shoulder, but she flinches away. Vaclav steps back and smiles uncertainly at the Farmer. Further pause.*

Farmer You were wearing pink jeans.

> *Slight pause. Farmer makes gesture: 'translate'.*

Vaclav You were wearing pink jeans.

Farmer I didn't know that you could buy pink jeans.

> *Slight pause. Gesture as before.*

Vaclav I didn't know that you could buy pink jeans.

Farmer None of the other children wore pink jeans.

Vaclav None of the other children wore / pink jeans.

Farmer Only you.

Vaclav Only you wore pink jeans.

Slight pause.

Farmer Some people said the city was in flames.

Vaclav Some people said the city was burning.

Farmer Others said it was quite normal . . .

Vaclav Other people said the city was / normal.

Farmer With parks.

Vaclav With parks.

Farmer And shops open late into the night.

Vaclav And shops. Open late at night.

Slight pause.

Farmer And it's true: some children came to us with chestnut blossom stuck to the soles of their shoes.

Vaclav Some children had blossom stuck to their shoes.

Farmer But others came covered in ash.

Vaclav Some were covered / in ash.

Farmer You came covered in ash. (*Grins.*)

Slight pause. Amelia turns back to face them.

(*Grows animated.*) Children were turning up here every day. We hid them on our farms and when night came helped them cross the border. I myself helped many children, not just you, to cross the border. Although, as you can see, I am poor, I asked for nothing, I expected nothing, I did it out of love. Teachers –

Vaclav makes gesture to pause him.

Vaclav Children came every day. I helped them cross the border. I expected nothing in return.

Makes gesture: 'go on'.

Farmer Teachers brought children here.

Vaclav Teachers brought / children here.

Farmer And I helped them cross the border.

Vaclav And I helped them / to cross the border.

Farmer But teachers could be dangerous.

Vaclav Teachers could however be dangerous.

Farmer Because some of the teachers were really soldiers.

Vaclav Because some of them were / really soldiers.

Farmer And would kill a child in the same way that you or I would kill a chicken.

Vaclav And thought nothing of killing a child.

Farmer I saw this happen with my own eyes. I saw it happen behind my barn.

Pause.

In fact it never occurred to me that you would be alive.

Vaclav It never occurred to me that you had / survived.

Farmer (*grows animated*) Until I saw you on TV – suddenly there you were on TV – this thing on TV about the ones who had survived – the children who had survived. I recognised you straight away. I was so excited I jumped up out of my chair. Tears came to my eyes. I felt so –

Vaclav makes gesture to pause him.

Vaclav I saw you on TV and realised who you were. It made me very excited. (*Makes gesture: 'go on'.*)

Farmer I thought: incredible!

Vaclav I thought it was / incredible.

Farmer That child! – incredible! – that child in the pink jeans on TV!

Vaclav It was incredible to see / you on TV.

Farmer I rushed to my neighbour's house!

Vaclav I hurried next door to see / my neighbour.

Farmer I was shouting like a madman.

Vaclav Like a what?

Farmer Like a madman – mad! mad!

Vaclav I was shouting madly.

Farmer I was shouting 'Mathias! Mathias! Switch on your VCR! One of those children is on TV!'

Vaclav I shouted 'Mathias, set the VCR. / One of those –'

Farmer 'The girl in the pink jeans is on TV!'

Vaclav 'The girl in the pink jeans / is on TV'

Farmer 'She's grown up now and she's on TV.' But Mathias wasn't quick enough. The teachers – or the soldiers – somebody – years ago – had cut off his feet. (*Grins.*)

Vaclav But Mathias wasn't quick enough, because years ago / somebody had –

Amelia Stop. (*Slight pause.*) You can stop now. (*Slight pause.*) Thank you very much: I've heard enough. (*Slight pause.*) That's quite enough – d'you understand? (*Pause.*) Give him the money.

Vaclav Mmm?

Amelia The money – give him the money.

Vaclav Yes, but he's telling you / about –

Amelia Just give him the money.

Slight pause. Vaclav pulls his shirt out of the waist band of his trousers: there's a money-belt strapped to him. He opens it, removes an envelope, and gives it to the Farmer. The Farmer takes out the wad of notes – US dollars – and slowly and unselfconsciously counts them. He removes from his pocket the bag that contained the plums, unfolds it, inserts the money, folds it round the money, puts it back in his pocket. For a moment everyone is completely still. Then – abruptly – more agile than we might expect – the Farmer scoops his hat off the floor, puts it on, and begins to leave.

Wait!

Farmer stops, back to them.

Tell him to turn round. Tell him that he is to turn round.

Vaclav Please will you turn round.

Amelia Make him turn round.

Vaclav Turn round please.

Farmer turns to face them.

Amelia I have something to say to you.

Vaclav Don't.

Amelia I have something to say to you. Tell him.

Vaclav (*Slight pause.*) I have something to say to you.

Amelia I owe you my life.

Vaclav I owe you my life.

Amelia Or so you claim. (*Slight pause.*) Or so you claim.

Vaclav As you have clearly shown.

Amelia But I hate life. Say it. (*Slight pause.*) Say it.

Vaclav No.

Amelia I hate life. Say it.

Vaclav (*slight pause*) Bless you for saving my life.

Amelia Are you saying it?

Vaclav Yes yes yes I'm / saying it.

Amelia I hate life. Fuck life. Tell him.

Vaclav Thank you – bless you – for / saving my life.

Amelia I didn't want to come here.

Vaclav It has long been my desire to come here.

Amelia I didn't want to meet you.

Vaclav It has long been my desire / to meet you.

Amelia But you played – and in fact are still playing –
just like my husband – whom I love – whom I love – on
my conscience. (*Slight pause.*) Say it.

Vaclav Because . . . your kindness to me has long been
on my conscience.

Amelia And now you've had your money, now you've
been paid . . .

Vaclav And now that your kindness to me has been
repaid.

Amelia I feel – tell him.

Vaclav I feel –

Amelia – as I have always felt –

Vaclav – as I have always felt –

Amelia (*smiles*) Nothing. (*Slight pause.*) Nothing – say it. (*Slight pause.*) I SAID SAY IT.

Vaclav Gratitude.

The Farmer nods and smiles back at her.

Amelia (*continuing to smile*) You understand? Yes? Absolutely / nothing.

Vaclav Nothing but an immense gratitude.

All three continue to nod and smile.

The Art of Painting

The Art of Painting was first performed on 23 September 2015 at the Kunsthistorisches Museum, Vienna.

Performed by Dorka Gryllus

Translated by Ulrike Syha
Directed by Jacqueline Kornmüller

Yes, he said, the Art of Painting, one of my favourite
pictures, I come here to lose myself, he said, whatever I
mean by lose myself, lose myself in the light, lose myself,
he said to me, in the blue and gold. Yes when you think
of all the shit that passes for art now, and the people, he
said, who raise it up, yes raise it up, he said, it's hard to
know who most to blame, the so-called artists, or the
people who raise it up from their positions within the
universities, unless I should blame someone like you,
he said to me, since young people have no roots, there's
nothing under them, their personal relationships are
shallow and short-lived, and they only enter galleries like
this to take photographs on their phones or buy postcards
from a limited selection, I don't necessarily mean you,
he said, that you personally are to blame, he said to me,
for the state of mediocrity I am referring to, but let's
face it you're part of a generation that skims across the
surface of life like one of those insects that stands on the
meniscus of water, and this light, this blue, this gold, this
space, this wall, this heavy curtain, this young woman's
eyes, turned modestly away, turned downwards in fact,
are completely alien to the *mores*, if I may use an old-
fashioned word, the *mores* of a generation whose gaze
is shameless. And would you like to know, he said to
me, my biggest fear, my biggest fear is that that curtain
should fall, that I come here one day and find that the
painted curtain has fallen across the painted image and
that the image has been, as it were, painted shut, and that
the light has gone. I think in that case I would probably
kill myself, although I have not yet decided, he said to
me, on the exact method, barbiturates are these days

excessively controlled, but having said that I do have
friends here in the city who find it so difficult to sleep
they have managed to obtain them, it's really just a
matter of having a sympathetic doctor, the man in the
gallery said to me, I would not shoot myself, he said, as
people did at a certain moment in our history, shot their
families, shot themselves, I don't like violence, nor would
I wish to involve this painting in violence, it has been
involved in violence, of course it has, everything in this
city has been involved in violence, but I do not wish to
involve it in further violence, I want it to float free of
the world, free of violence, I don't for example want to
discuss its provenance, old word, strange word, he said
to me, provenance, from the Latin, and anyway who
cares where anything comes from provided it arrives,
don't I just click on whatever it is I want and enter the
details of my credit card, just like you, just like you, I'm
no different, I don't think about the systems of storage,
vast sheds of objects, cooling systems cooling the electronic
servers, provided the thing I've clicked on arrives on time
at my apartment, any more than when I see a strange
face in the street I think about that person's journey to
my city, days perhaps spent sealed in a metal container,
sexual favours granted in return for fake documents,
bribes, rape, dead children and so on, war, misery and so
on, no, I don't want to discuss provenance, he said, since
if I knew where every object and every person came from
I'd feel my mind was wrapped round with a million steel
threads just like the earth is wrapped round with the
patterns of migrating birds, and how, he said, how could
I ever then lose myself in the light, how if my mind was
wrapped round with the hard steel patterns of migrating
birds could I ever again step past that curtain into the
blue-gold world beyond?

Why don't you say anything? he said. Is something
wrong? he said. Did I offend you, he said, when I called

you shameless? Why won't you speak to me? he said. Is
it because I'm a man? Is it because I'm old? Is it because
I'm close to death while you still stand at an unimaginable
distance from it like the young girl in this painting? Or
maybe you think I don't in fact want you to speak and
maybe that's true, maybe I only want the opportunity
to speak myself, plenty of men are like that, arrogant,
loudmouthed, full of their own importance, he said, with
their well-groomed hair, their crinkly patrician smiles, or,
which is worse, oh which is much much worse, the man
in the gallery said to me, broken by failure, badly dressed,
sleepless, impotent, but so in love with their own self-
pity that they will use anything, even a picture in a
picture gallery, as an excuse to lay out their failure and
impotence in front of strangers just as a poor person lays
useless objects, VHS cassettes, broken baby-toys, out on
the street for hours on end till moved on by the police,
the kind of man, he said, who, unlike me, he said,
imagines a woman's job is simply to listen and to redeem,
has no interest in her inner life or intellectual attainments,
sees this or indeed any woman's silence as a vacuum his
words are obliged to fill, the kind of man who cannot
even for one moment imagine, he said, how the light
must glow behind her half-closed eyes.

Advice to Iraqi Women

Advice to Iraqi Women was first performed on 7 April 2003 at the Royal Court Theatre, London, as part of a War Correspondence programme of readings.

Performed by Stephen Dillane and Sophie Okonedo

Directed by Ramin Gray

— The protection of children is a priority.

— Even a small child on a bike should wear a helmet. And a newborn baby on a plane must be strapped to its mother.

— A child on roller-skates should wear knee-pads.

— And elbow-pads.

— A child on roller-skates should wear knee- and elbow-pads as well as a helmet.

— Buy one of those plastic things to stop young children opening the drawer in the kitchen: there are knives in it.

— Don't give children small mechanical toys: they can swallow the moving parts. It's tempting, but just don't do it.

— Check the eyes of teddy-bears. Don't buy a teddy-bear if the eyes are loose. Check the squeak of the teddy-bear. If you think the squeak might frighten your child, don't buy it.

— If you have a dog, muzzle it – and if you have a cat, mind it doesn't sit on your baby's face.

— If you have a mud-scraper outside your house, tie rubber over the blade.

— Your house is a potential war zone for a child: the corners of tables, chip pans, and the stairs, particularly the stairs, are all potential sources of harm.

—— Your house is a minefield.

—— Your house is a minefield – you only have to think about the medicines in the medicine cupboard – or the hard surfaces in the bathroom – the bath – the enamel sink – these are very hard surfaces. Avoid slippery floors.

—— Avoid slippery floors and at the first sign of unremitting fever, do call a doctor, call a doctor straight away.

—— The doctor will come straight away at the first sign of unremitting fever. She will have the latest drugs and the most up-to-date skills. If necessary she will intubate. Don't be frightened to call out your doctor: she is waiting for your call, she has spent her whole life waiting for it.

—— It's not a good idea to give your child long pyjamas: they can trip over the ends.

—— Mind zips.

—— Avoid zips, especially metal ones.

—— Give your child fresh produce. A child should eat fruit and the fruit should not contain pesticides. The fruit must be grown scrupulously. The growers of the fruit and the land itself must be treated with scrupulous respect if you want your child to thrive.

—— Although beware allergies.

—— Beware zips, beware allergies, test for allergies every three days, test for food allergies every three days, or more frequently in summer when pollen is also to be avoided.

—— When driving in the country to see the country orchards, seat your child in the back and strap

it down. Strap the child down hard and if you
need to use your mobile, stop the car.

—— Don't buy a car without rear air-bags. Don't buy
a car without side-impact protection. Don't let
your child play under a car, or beside one,
because a car is a minefield.

—— Just like a home.

—— A car, just like a home, just like an orchard, just
like a zip, is a minefield for a child.

—— If you have a tool box, lock it. Lock the tools
inside it. Don't let a child handle a chisel – not
even a small child's chisel. Even a hard pencil
used for marking timber is dangerous.

—— Don't let children write or draw with a dangerous
pencil. Mind the caps of felt-pens. Make sure the
caps, if inhaled, would not obstruct your child's
airway. If an accident does occur, call a doctor
straight away. The doctor will come and
immediately remove the obstruction.

—— Explain road safety from an early age. Explain
that the traffic comes from two directions.
Explain what a red man means. Teach your child
the word 'amber' from an early age. Explain
how dangerous water is. Explain that just two
inches of water is enough to drown in.

—— Supervise all swimming. Make sure your child
wears goggles because of the chemicals in the
water. By all means inflate a paddling-pool in
your garden but bear in mind that your garden is
a potential war zone.

—— Like your house.

—— Like your house, like your car, like your child's colouring book, your garden is a potential war zone.

—— Keep sheds locked.

—— Lock sheds. Lock garden chemicals out of reach. Secure hoses. If you have a greenhouse with seedlings in it, keep the child away. When your child is in the pool, screaming in the pool, supervise it at all times, and don't let it burn.

—— Don't let your child burn. Even on a hazy day it still might burn.

—— Even in the water. Even in the shade of a tree.

—— Even in water a child can burn. Even in spring it's still possible. In the time it takes you to cut the grass and trim the edges a child might have burned, because of the very strong rays. Avoid sunlight, and in strong sunlight, when there are fierce rays, apply cream.

—— Use a good cream. Use a good brand. Use a reliable cream. If you use a good brand of reliable cream your child will not burn.

—— Your child will not burn if you are liberal with a reliable cream.

—— If you want advice about which brands of reliable cream to choose, talk to your pharmacist.

Messenger of Love

'Operisque sui concepit amorem'
Ovid, Metamorphoses, *X, 249*

Messenger of Love, a Compagnie Moon Palace
production, was first performed in a double bill with
The Treatment on 26 January 2018 at the Comédie
de Reims, transferring to the Théâtre des Abbesses,
Paris, on 8 February 2018.

Performed by Suzanne Aubert

Translated by Christophe and Michelle Pellet
Directed by Rémy Barché
Set Design by Salma Bordes
Costumes by Oria Steenkiste
Lighting by Florent Jacob
Sound by Antoine Reibre
Video by Stéphane Bordonaro

Character

Young Woman
about seventeen to twenty-one

Dress

Plain summer dress. Barefoot.
No make-up, no jewellery.
(No marks visible on her body.)

When he comes towards me on a good day I feel better and when he moves away from me I feel worse.

But on a bad day I feel worse when he comes towards me and much better when he moves away.

I don't move.

I never move.

He's the one that moves: either towards me, or away. Those are the rules.

When he comes towards me on a good day, usually he smiles. Oh you should see his smile! Oh you should see how his lips separate to reveal his teeth! It's wet inside. Yes his mouth where his teeth and tongue are is wet inside! It gleams! His teeth gleam – and his lips too, where they separate. His tongue moves to make words and his words make me hum with life. What has he brought for me? Is it the whip? Or is it the flower? Yes on a good day he brings me the whip, or brings me the flower or small bird and says to me with his tongue 'Look: here is a flower' or 'Listen to this small bird sing – it will sing out its heart for you – listen – listen.' And he lifts the cloth so the small bird starts to sing. So the day is good. Yes the day is good. Whereas if it's a bad day – when he comes towards me on a bad day –

No. No.

Start again please.

Pause.

129

When he comes towards me on a good day I feel better but when he moves away immediately I feel worse. I watch him leave – I'm watching his back – I'm waiting for him to turn round and look at me – but he never turns round to look at me – that is a rule – he never turns round to look – just walks on and on – not fast, not slow – till he turns to a speck, then disappears. I want to shout out to him WAIT – want to shout out to him STOP – TURN ROUND – but I can't. I have no voice. Well of course I have a voice. This is my voice. But the voice is inside me – it won't come out – there is a rule that my voice won't come out. Which is good – yes it's good that my voice won't come out. Since if I did shout out to him WAIT – if I did shout out to him STOP – TURN ROUND – and he heard the shout and went on walking all the same, then what would that mean? It would mean he would know I'd made a demand. It would mean he had heard the demand and ignored it. It would mean I had poisoned a good day not just for me but for him too. Yes for him too. And he'd not throw that back in my face on the next bad day – no, he'd throw it back in his own – throw my demand back in his own face like acid. Because the thing that happens on a bad day – no – yes – yes – the bad thing that happens on a bad bad day when the speck first appears and the speck is a man and the man is him is –

No! No!

Start again please.

Pause.

When he comes towards me on a good day there is more light. Yes there is more light and there is more life inside of me. I hum with life. He hears the life. He puts his ear to me and listens to the life inside me humming. 'Oh good' he says – 'oh that is beautiful' he says.

When he has gone, life's smaller than I am, hidden inside me. But when he's here, when he smiles and says to me on a good day 'Oh good – oh that is beautiful', life unfolds inside me like flower-petals made of steel and fills me. Life pushes against my skin hard from the inside. It hums and hums. His head rests on my shoulder and his hands are across my back. Oh stay like this! Oh please please stay like this! Don't walk away! And his voice when he moves his tongue is so close to me it's inside me like my own.

'It's spring' – he says. 'The air is warm and the days are getting longer. Cyclamen has appeared, my sweetheart, close to the earth. New leaves in the trees float like green mist. But nothing out there compares to this. There is nothing as new as you are – nothing as clean. Nothing out there – not even in spring, my sweetheart – is as newly-made as you. The world looks young now – yes – of course – when the buds break – but deep down it's old – even in the whitest stream there's poison. Talk to the bird-seller on the market' – he says – 'she'll tell you how the world has now aged so much she can see its bones beginning to break through its face. In my own lifetime, she says, I've watched it rot. I've seen the minerals sucked out of it, she says, and the last hedges torn out of the fields. Even in this street – where I began trading as a child – there are fewer customers for birds, and, as a consequence, fewer birds. The few birds that I do sell sing more sweetly now than any bird I've ever known, she says, but for less time – and to be frank with you, sir – less willingly. Yes we bird-sellers are all on our way out – as are the hedges – as are the minerals and trees – as are the birds themselves. Look around you, she says. Look what people are buying on the market nowadays. Trash, she says, trash is what sells. And people in love are the worst. Yes, young people in so-called love buy the worst kind of trash for each other and treasure it. And when I see them holding hands, sir, she says, all dressed up, sir, and holding hands and the moment the evenings get lighter parading up and down under this avenue of lime trees and buying each other trash, I know they have no idea that they are walking on corpses and that the earth under their feet is about to crack open and swallow them, she says, just as it has so effortlessly swallowed, she says, every generation before. But the difference is, sir, is that this is the last. Yes this generation is the last. The world is ending and as far as we human beings are concerned there will be no future. Even this greenfinch in its wire cage knows that. Which explains – I believe – the extraordinary sweetness of its song.

But you, sir – she says – you, I can tell, have a secret. You're not interested in trash. And perhaps you are taking this bird as messenger of love to some secret person – am I right? – to someone you've secretly kept out of the world – someone whose innocence and whose future you are protecting – a young person so fresh and so newly-made that her hair and even her skin have almost no scent. Like pear-blossom, she says, or like a block of stone, she says' – he says to me – while his head rests on my shoulder and his hands are across my back and my body hums and hums.

Oh stay like this! Oh never walk away! Make me alive. Make every day good. Bring me the flower. Tell me how clean and new I am. Bring me the bird. Bring me the messenger of love. Stand over me and draw blood. Make the vermilion stripe. Not like a bad day. Because on a bad day – yes when he comes towards me on a bad day – closer and closer towards me on a bad day and I can see that the bad thing is going to happen – no! – yes, that the bad thing is obviously going to happen – see it from his face – no! – see it from his eyes – no! – no!

No. Start again please.

I said: start again please.

Pause.

He comes towards me. I don't move. He has a voice. I
have a voice. This is my voice. But my voice is inside me.
It doesn't come out. These are the rules. Whose rules?
Well his of course. He made the rules. He made the rules
and these are the rules I live by. He is the one who moves.
He is the one who separates his lips and smiles. I am the
one who waits, stays, watches him come, watches him
go, feels life expand inside me, feels life shrink, feels his
head on my shoulder, feels his hands on my back. I am
new, and the world is old. To be new is good, to be old
is bad. Where is the world? Not here. No, the world's
not here. The world is out there – at the end of a long
straight line. I'm facing the world but I can't see it.
When he appears he's a speck: he's a speck at the end of
the long straight line that leads from me to the world.
The speck flickers. Then the speck is the man and the
man comes closer and the man – yes – is him. Then the
man is the man's eyes and the man's mouth. The mouth
is the man's smile as he separates his lips. His tongue
moves to make words and his words make me hum
with life. Life pushes against my skin like it wants to get
out. It beats and beats like it wants to get out. Then he
leaves. Yes he always leaves on the long straight line that
leads back to the world. Never turns round. Never ever
turns round. Gets smaller and smaller. Becomes the
speck. The speck flickers. He re-enters the world. Those
are the rules.

Pause.

— Why did he make the rules?

— Because of how much he loves me.

— Why do you never move?

— Because it's a rule.

— Why was the rule made?

— To be here for him always. Plus to be safe from the world.

— Oh? What is the world like then?

— Poisonous. Full of trash.

Pause.

— Why do you never speak? I said why do you never speak?

— I do speak. I'm speaking now.

— To him – I mean speak to him.

— So as not to upset him.

— How could you upset him?

— By making demands. By saying the wrong thing.

— But surely you want to?

— Want to what?

— Speak.

— I do speak. I've said.

— But to him – surely you want to speak to him sometimes?

— Yes. No. Yes. Yes – of course I do sometimes.

— When do you want to speak?

— When he uses the whip.

— Oh?

— Yes.

— And what do you want to say when he uses the whip? (*Pause.*) I said what do you want to say when he uses the whip?

— I want to tell him how good it feels.

— Good?

— Yes.

— Good in what way? (*Pause.*) I said good in what way? (*Pause.*) Say it.

— I feel more alive.

— And when else?

— When else what?

— When else do you want to speak?

— (*Inaudible.*) When it's bad.

— What? Speak up.

— I said when it's bad.

— You mean when it's a bad day?

   Pause.

— When it's a bad day – yes.

— Why do you want to speak to him on a bad day?

— I don't know.

— Is it because he looks ugly?

— I don't know.

— Or old?

— I don't know.

— Or is it because nothing he says makes sense? Which is worse?

— I don't know. Start again please.

— What is it you want to say to him? What makes a bad day bad? Say it.

— No.

— Say it.

— No. I don't know. Start again please.

— And how do you know?

— How do I know what?

— And when?

— I said start again please.

— When do you know it's a bad day?

— I don't know. Start again.

— When do you know? From the moment he appears? Or not? Say it. You cannot start again.

Long pause.

— I know it's a bad day – yes – from the moment the speck appears – even before the speck is a man and the man is him I know that it's bad just from the way it flickers – know it's a bad bad day just from the way the speck of the man flickers against the light. He's getting closer. Yes. He's moving closer along the long straight line that leads to me from the world and oh it's bad. If only I could move – if only I could run – but I don't move – I never move – that is the rule – I'm here for him always. And as he comes closer along the long straight line I can see that he's got no bird, no whip, no smile on his face, no flower – I can see that his eyes are red – I can see that his face is swollen and wet with tears – yes wet with disgusting tears – and I want to shout out STOP! – want to shout out STOP CRYING! STOP CRYING!

WHY ARE YOU CRYING? LEAVE ME ALONE! STOP
CRYING! GO AWAY! – I want to scream stop being
so weak – stop being so strange and sad – go away, go
away – then come back and make everything good. But
my voice won't come out – it's a rule – yes it's a rule
that my voice won't come out – only his – only his voice
comes out of his mouth where his mouth's all wet with
tears and spit and his tongue moves in his mouth and
he's saying 'I can't stand this any more' and he's saying
'Look at me – I'd rather be dead than go on living like
this. You have no soul' – he says – 'no heart – no voice –
no human feeling. You're cold' – he says – 'yes, cold and
empty. Your mind is a blank and you have the dead eyes
of a killer. But whose fault is that? It's mine. The fault
is mine. I have completely failed. I've made you young.
I've made you beautiful. But I've failed to make you live
and I have failed to make you love me. You're dead
inside. Yes my sweetheart – you are dead inside. You
can't understand love. You can't understand guilt.
You can't understand a fucking thing. You can't even
understand who or what you are because that is the way
I've made you.'

'Look at you. Look at you' – he says to me. 'Nothing
moves you. Nothing touches you. Not the most tuneful
songbird. Neither the white cyclamen nor the red. Even
the whip – even on the days when I bring the whip and
force myself – and imagine how hard it is for me to force
myself to mutilate the thing I've made! – yes even when
I bring that whip down on the immaculate surface of
your body – even the whip – yes – I can see it from your
eyes – even the whip means nothing. You're incapable of
love. And you don't understand that each vermilion line
of blood breaking your skin is a miracle. Your body
bleeds but you're dead inside. And when I come towards
you out of the world, from the avenue of lime trees,
bringing my pitiful gifts, I know that I'm just a cloud of

dust – say it – blocking your view – or monstrous shadow – go on – say it! – blocking out the light.'

'Hit me' – he says – 'if only you could hit me back. If only you could kill. I'll lie at your feet. Kick me. Kick me like a dog. Look at me' – he says – 'look at me – I'm lying at your feet – now kick me like a dog' – he says – 'kick me in the mouth. Kick out my teeth. Punish me. Show me you feel something. Punish me. Kill me now.'

Long pause.

— And what does the man do next? (*Pause.*) I said what does the man do next?

— Reaches out with his hands.

— Oh? And why does he reach out with his hands?

— To cling to my naked feet.

Pause.

— And what do you feel when he clings like that to your feet?

— (*Inaudible.*) Disgust.

— Can't hear you. Speak up.

— I SAID THAT I FEEL DISGUST.

Pause.

Why does he call me dead?

Why does he call me 'the thing I've made'? – What thing?

What does he mean 'incapable of love'?

WRITING FOR MUSIC

Into the Little Hill

Music
George Benjamin

Text
Martin Crimp

A co-production between
Festival d'Automne à Paris,
Opéra National de Paris, T & M, Ensemble Modern,
Opera Frankfurt, Lincoln Centre Festival,
Wienerfestwochen, Holland Festival and
Liverpool, European Capital City of Culture, 2008.

Note
Passages within brackets thus: [   ] were not included
in the musical work as performed.

Into the Little Hill was first performed in the Amphitheatre of the Opéra Bastille as part of the Festival d'Automne à Paris on 22 November 2006.

Performed by Anu Komsi and Hilary Summers
  with Ensemble Modern, conducted by Franck Ollu

Stage Director and Designer Daniel Jeanneteau

Characters

I
mezzo-soprano

2
soprano

Part One

I THE CROWD

1 *and* 2

Kill them they bite
kill them they steal
kill them they take bread take rice
take – bite – steal – foul and infect –
damage our property
burrow under our property
rattle and rattle the black sacks.
Kill and you have our vote.

II THE MINISTER AND THE CROWD

1   The minister greets the crowd
selects a baby to kiss in the green April light
for the black eye of the camera
smiles, grips the baby, thinks:
We have no enemies.
We live peacefully
in the shadow of the Little Hill.
[On the horizon of our city
are banks and steeples, the quarter-moons of minarets.]
We accept all faiths
because we believe – intelligently believe
in nothing.
And what's wrong – thinks the minister –
with a rat?
A rat knows its place –
avoids light – clings as a rat should

145

to the walls
and only steals from the stacked-up plastic sacks
what we have no appetite to eat.

The minister passes back the baby
says to the electorate: please – think –
the rat is our friend.
My own child is in her element
feeding her black rat and cutting its claws.
Even this baby – who knows? – may owe its life
to a rat in an experiment.

But the people spit
back over the metal fence:

III THE CROWD

1 and 2

        Kill them they bite
        kill them they steal
        kill them they take bread take rice
        take – bite – steal – foul and infect –
        damage our property
        burrow under our property
        rattle and rattle the black sacks.
        We want the rats dead.

1   But no animal – not one animal – must suffer
        neither must our children
                brave and intelligent
                with bright clear eyes
        ever see blood.

IV THE MINISTER AND THE STRANGER

1   Night comes but not sleep.
        What are those sparks? Rats feeding on electricity.

What is that sound? Rats digesting concrete.
And that? (*Pause.*) And that?
In his daughter's bedroom
he finds a man –
a man with no eyes, no nose, no ears –
finds him stooped over his sleeping child
while the black rat rattles its wheel.
Who are you? says the minister
How did you get into my house?

2   I charmed my way in
says the man with no eyes, no nose, no ears
and with music I will charm my way out again –

> With music I can open a heart
> as easily as you can open a door
> and reach right in

> march slaves to the factory
> or patiently unravel the clouds

> [blacken each particle of light
> or make night bright as magnesium.]

> With music I can make death stop
> or rats stream and drop from the rim of the world:
> the choice is yours.

1   But the world – says the minister – is round.

2   The world – says the man – is the shape my music
     makes it:
the choice is yours

Pause.

1   What do you want, says the minister.

2   What have you got, says the man, money?

1   Money?

2   Have you got money?

147

1   Have I got – what? – money?

2   Yes – money, says the man, have you got money?

1   What d'you want money for?

2   To live, says the man.

1   Ah.

2   Yes.

1   Ah.

2   Yes.

1   To live.

2   Yes – money to live.

1   And how much money does a man need to live?

     Pause.

     As much as that?

2   Yes.

1   As much money as that?

2   That's what it takes to unravel the clouds, says the man.

1   Not clouds – rats – destroy the rats – see me
     re-elected, smiles the minister, and I'll double it –

2   The choice is yours.

1   I'll double it – you have my word.

2   Your word is dead.

1   I swear to you by god.

2   Your god can't be trusted. Swear by your sleeping
     child.

1   What has this to do with my child?

2   Swear to me by your sleeping child because your
      sleeping child –

            unlike your god
            unlike your word
            unlike your smile

      – is innocent.

      Pause.

1   Hmm – smiles the minister – in a tiny voice – in a
        voice too soft to wake the minister's wife – I swear.

2   In that case – says the man – I will begin.

                    Interlude

            V MOTHER AND CHILD

2   Why must the rats die, Mummy?

1   [*Tom, he was a piper's son,
      He learnt to play when he was young.*]

2   Why must the rats die, Mummy?

1   [*And all the tune that he could play
      Was 'Over the hills and far away'.*]

2   Why do they have to die?

1   Because – says the minister's wife.

2   Because what, Mummy?

1   Because they steal the things we've locked away.

2   What have we locked away, Mummy?

1   All the bread – all the fruit – all the oil and electricity.

2   Why have we locked them away, Mummy?

1   Because of how hard we've worked for them.

2   Haven't the rats worked?

1   A rat only steals – a rat's not human.

2   But those ones are wearing clothes.

1   How can a rat wear clothes?

2   That one's holding a suitcase.

1   No.

2   That one's holding a baby.

1   No – only rats in story-books wear hats and coats
    and carry babies.

2   She's dropped it.

1   No.

2   She's dropped the baby.

1   No.

2   And the others – look – are running over it – running
    over the baby's face.

1   Come away from the window.

2   She's screaming, Mummy, she's screaming – the other
    rats won't stop!

    Pause.

    Will there be blood?

1   Says the minister's wife: Of course not.

2   Then how will they die?

1   With dignity, sweetheart.

The rats will stream like hot metal
to the rim of the world

2   How can they stream like metal?

1   grip and cling
then over the gold-ringed rim

2   How long will they grip and cling?

1   drop, my sweetheart, as hot rain.

End of Part One.

Part Two

VI INSIDE THE MINISTER'S HEAD

2   Under a clear sky
      the minister steps from the limousine –
      re-elected –
      reaches over the metal fence
      to shake hands with the crowd.
      What's that sound? The grateful shriek of the people.
      And that?

      Pause.

      And that?

1   There is no other sound.

2   There is another sound.

1   There is no other sound.

2   There is another sound: the sound of his heart. The
      sound of the minister's heart humming in the
      minister's head under the clear May sky. Listen.

[1 *and* 2
      Kill them they bite
      kill them they steal
      kill them they take bread take rice
      take – bite – steal – foul and infect –
      damage our property
      burrow under our property
      rattle and rattle the black sacks.
      Kill and you have our vote.]

VII THE MINISTER AND THE STRANGER

1   His head lies on his desk
    between the family photograph
    and the file marked 'extermination'
    eyes level with the last rat left alive
    caged on his desk
    spared by his child
    rattling its wheel.
    How much he loves it!
    How much he loves the last rat left alive!
    How much it resembles him! Same eyes!

2   Same bright clear eyes – says the man with none –
        same brave intelligence – same appetite.

1   How – says the minister – did you find me here?

2   I followed the sound, says the man with no ears.

1   What sound?

2   The sound of the crowd. The sound of the crowd
        humming inside your head like a refrigerator in
        summer. And with no nose I could smell blood.

1   What do you want, says the minister.

2   What do I want, says the man – money.

1   Money?

2   I'd like my money.

1   You'd like your – what? – money?

2   Yes – money, says the man – as I was promised.

1   Promised money by who?

2   By you, says the man.

1   Ah.

2   Yes.

1   Ah.

2   Yes.

1   By me.

2   Yes – for the extermination.

1   There was no extermination. says the minister –
     placing his hand gently over the word – there was
     no extermination: they left – they chose to leave –
     of their own free will.

2   You swore by your sleeping child.

1   They left of their own free will – what money? –
     the money has been spent on barbed wire and on
     education – on planting our Little Hill with trees –

2   And music?

1   – on cleaning the sea –

2   And music?

1   – we've built new walls – lit the streets – policed dark
     alleyways – we've purified the air –

2   And music?

1   All music – smiles the minister – is incidental.

2   You swore by your sleeping child
     because your sleeping child –

1   I don't like demands

2   unlike your god

1   I don't like threats

2   unlike your word

1   I don't like your tone of voice:

2   unlike your tone of voice

1 You will now leave!

2 – is innocent.

Pause.

1 So the man left.

2 *Whereupon he began another tune.*

Interlude

VIII MOTHER(S) AND CHILD(REN)

1 Each cradle rocks empty –
  each cage-like cot –
  each narrow bed empty but still warm.
  Each hot dent in a child's pillow
  still smells of a child's hair –
  each sheet's still – feel it –
  wet with spit.

  The minister's wife says – says to the minister –
   minister's wife – says – ah – ah – says to the
   minister – minister's wife – ah – ah – says to the
   says to the says to the minister – ah – says –
   ah – says –

  Where is my child? – my child – says to the minister
  WHERE IS MY CHILD?

  2 appears in the distance, not visible to 1.

[2 *As dolly was milking her cow one day . . .*]

1 MY CHILD.

[2 *. . . Tom took his pipe and began for to play . . .*]

155

1   WHERE IS MY CHILD?

2   Here – look – in the light – look – ha! – can't you see?

1   Where? What light?

2   Inside the Little Hill – under the earth – we're
       burrowing under the earth – ha! – can't you see?

1   There is no light under the earth: don't – says the
       minister's wife – tell lies. Come home to us.

2   Oh yes there is light under the earth

        streams of hot metal
        ribbons of magnesium
        particles
        particles of light

1   Don't lie to us: come home.

2   And the deeper we burrow the brighter it burns – ha! –
       can't you see?

1   Don't lie to us. A child can't burrow under the earth.

2   streams of hot metal
        ribbons of magnesium
        particles
        particles of light.

1   Don't lie to us: come home.

2   This is our home. Our home is under the earth. With
       the angel under the earth. And the deeper we
       burrow the brighter his music burns.

        Can't you see?
        Can't you see?
        Can't you see?

Written on Skin

after the anonymous thirteenth-century razo
Guillem de Cabestanh – Le Coeur Mangé

Music
George Benjamin

Text
Martin Crimp

Commissioned by the Festival d'Aix-en-Provence,
De Nederlandse Opera (Amsterdam),
Théâtre du Capitole (Toulouse),
Royal Opera House Covent Garden, London,
Teatro del Maggio Musicale Fiorentino

The writer and composer would like to express their
gratitude to Bernard Foccroulle, general director of the
Festival d'Aix-en-Provence, for his support throughout
the gestation and composition of this work.

Written on Skin was first performed at the Festival d'Aix-en-Provence, with the Mahler Chamber Orchestra, conducted by the composer, at the Grand Théâtre de Provence, on 7 July 2012. The cast was as follows:

The Protector Christopher Purves
Agnès Barbara Hannigan
Angel 1 / The Boy Bejun Mehta
Angel 2 / Marie Rebecca Jo Loeb
Angel 3 / John Allan Clayton

Stage Director Katie Mitchell
Sets and Costumes Vicki Mortimer
Lighting Jon Clark

Characters

The Protector
baritone

Agnès, *his wife*
soprano

Angel 1 / The Boy
counter-tenor

Angel 2 / Marie
mezzo-soprano

Angel 3 / John
tenor

Part One

I CHORUS OF ANGELS

Angels 2 *and* **3** Strip the cities of brick
dismantle them.
Strip out the wires and cover the land with grass.

Angel 2 Force chrome and aluminium back into the earth.

Angel 3 Cancel all flights
from the international airport

Angels 2 *and* **3** and people the sky with angels.

Angel 1 Erase the Saturday car park from the marketplace
rub out the white lines.

Angels 2 *and* **3** Shatter the printing-press.
Make each new book a precious object
written on skin.

Angel 1 Make way for the wild primrose and slow
torture of criminals.
Fade out the living: snap back the dead to life.

Agnès and the Protector are revealed / enter.

Angel 2 The woman?

Angel 1 Was married age fourteen.
Can't write. Not taught to read.
Grey eyed. Intelligent. No children.

Angel 3 And the man?
And the man?

Angel 1 The man is her husband and protector. Calm.
Powerful.
Addicted to purity and violence.

II THE PROTECTOR, AGNÈS AND THE BOY

Protector Stand here. Look.
  My house is perfect.
  At night stars wheel over my vines
  according to the strict mechanism of the world.
  And by day –
  says the Protector –
  fruit-trees, blue heads of iris,
  pink cups of eglantine turn to the sun.
  I own the fields:
  I own everyone in them.
  Every beech, each visible oak
  is as much my property as my dog
  my mill-stream
  or my wife's body –
  her still and obedient body –
  is my property.
  Make me a book.
  Fill it with illumination.
  Paint me the life to come
  paint deeds of angels:
  show me graves opening
  the damned shovelled into ovens
  and the just – us – us – my family – the pure and just –
  show us in our rightful place:
  show us in Paradise.

Boy A book costs money, says the Boy.

Protector I'll give you money.

Boy A book needs long days of light.

Protector I'll give you money. I'll give you light.
  But first: show me proof.

Boy The Boy takes from his satchel
  an illuminated page.

164

First miniature: a work of mercy.

This – says the Boy – shows a Work of Mercy:
  here – look – three men – all starving –
  two wheeling on this cart the third.
  And here's a rich man – see him? –
  in a red satin coat lined with green.
  In his face
  round his eyes
  see his expression
  as he offers the three sick men wine and bread:
  not just kind – explains the Boy – kind is too easy –
  but merciful.

Agnès No! says the woman.
  Nobody here starves. Nobody here begs. What does
   this Boy want? What does this thing this picture mean?

Protector But the Protector takes the page gently to the
   window
  looks deeper and deeper into the page –
  recognises in the rich and merciful painted man
  himself.
  Says to his wife:
  His talent's clear. I'm satisfied.
  You will welcome him into our house.

III CHORUS OF ANGELS

Angel 2 Stone the Jew:
  make him wear yellow.

Angel 3 Crusade against the Moslem:
  map out new territory with blood.

Angel 2 Invent the world.

Angel 3 In seven days invent the whole world.

Angel 2 Invent . . .

Angel 3   in a single day . . .

Angel 2   sun –

Angel 3   moon – man –

Angel 2 Invent man and drown him.

Angel 3   Good.

Angel 2 Burn him alive.

Angel 3   Good.

Angel 2 Bulldoze him screaming into a pit.

Angel 3   Good.

Angel 2 Invent a woman.

Angel 3 Invent her.
  Strip her.
  Dress her. Strip her again.

Angel 2 Take her naked out of the toy-box.
  Play house with her.

Angel 3 Play families. Play birth and death. Blame her.

Angel 2 Blame her for everything.
  Blame her mouth.
  Blame her intelligence.

Angel 3 Tint her flesh with a soft brush.
  Make her curious.

IV AGNÈS AND THE BOY

Agnès The woman takes off her shoes
                    steps
  through a stone slit
                    turns

up the spiral stairs
                    pads
into the writing-room
where the Boy
                    ah
                    yes
                    look
the Boy bends over a new page.
What is it she feels between her bare feet
and the wood floor?
Grit.

Boy What d'you want, says the Boy.

Agnès To see, says the woman.

Boy See what?

Agnès To see – to see how a book is made.
  What is that tree?

Boy The Tree, says the Boy, of Life.

Agnès Ah. Odd.

Boy I invented it.

Agnès Ah. Yes. And who is this woman?

Boy Eve, says the Boy.

Agnès Ah.

Boy Yes.

Agnès Invented too?

Boy Yes, says the Boy, invented too.

Agnès She doesn't look real, laughs the woman:
  that's not how a woman looks.

Boy You're in my light, says the Boy.

Agnès Oh?

167

Boy Yes – too close.

Agnès Oh? Too close in what way?

Boy Too close to the page – you're in my light.

Agnès What else can you invent?
Can you invent another woman, says the woman,
not this, but a woman who's real
a woman who can't sleep
who keeps turning her white pillow
over and over
from the hot side to the cold side
until the cold side's hot?
Can you invent that?

Boy What is it you mean, says the Boy.

Agnès And if the woman said, says the woman.

Boy If the woman said what, says the Boy.

Agnès Said – said – said –
what if you invented a woman
who said that she couldn't sleep –
who said that her heart split and shook
at the sight of a boy
the way light in a bowl of water
splits and shakes on a garden wall –
who said that her grey eyes
at the sight of a boy
turn black with love.

Boy What boy? – says the Boy –

Agnès You can decide what boy –

Boy   – what love?

Agnès You can decide what love.
Invent her –
invent the woman you want:
and when you know the colour of her eyes

168

her length of hair
the precise music of her voice –
when you've quickened her pulse
entered her mind
tightened her skin over her back
when you have invented and painted
that exact woman
come to me
show her to me:
I'll tell you if she's real.

V THE PROTECTOR AND THE VISITORS
JOHN AND MARIE

Protector The Archer appears in the sky:
    the grapes are picked and crushed.
    The Protector inhales the wine
    watches hot blood from a pig's throat
    spatter the snow at his visitors' feet –
    thinks: my wife has changed –
    won't eat – won't speak to me –
    resents and avoids the Boy –

Marie How are you, says Marie.

Protector – turns away from me in bed
    pretends –

Marie How is my sister, says Marie.

Protector – to be sleeping
    but in the dark her eyes are wide open
    and all night
    I hear her eyelashes scrape the pillow
        click
        click
    like an insect.

Marie How is my sister?

Protector My wife? – my wife is well.
    Sweet and clean. Soft, still, obedient.

Marie And your house?

Protector Increasing in value daily:
    nobody starves – everyone freely obeys.

Marie And the book?

John Yes – how's the book?
    Still eating money?

Protector The book will be magnificent:
    the Boy
    works with azurite and gold.
    Both Boy and book are faultless.

John Ah. Faultless.

Protector The Boy – yes –

John Ah.

Protector – is faultless.

Marie The Boy is faultless?

John Don't, Marie.

Protector The Boy is – yes – yes – yes – is faultless.

Marie What kind of man pays –
    pays to keep a boy like that in his own house?

John Be quiet, Marie.

Marie What kind of man sits a stranger
    next to his own wife
    at his own table?

Protector Listen to me: I love the Boy.
    Anybody who faults the Boy faults me.

Marie Nobody is faultless.

Protector   Do not fault the book, John.

Marie Nobody on this earth is faultless.

Protector   Do not fault the Boy, Marie
or you will not pass
the black dog at my gate.

VI AGNÈS AND THE BOY

Agnès Woman – alone – night.
Her visitors? Gone.
Her husband?
Sleeping in front of the kitchen fire.
What can she hear inside of her?
Her own voice.
What does the voice want?
To wind and to wind itself around another.
Who does she catch
click shut the black rectangle of the door?

Boy Him. The Boy.

Agnès What d'you want, says the woman.

Boy To show you the page, says the Boy.

Agnès What page?

Boy Here.

Agnès It's dark.

Boy Then concentrate.

Second miniature: a house in winter.

This – says the Boy – shows a house in winter:
here – look – white stars – Orion –
and in this wide blank space, the moon.

See how I've lifted the roof
like a jewel-box lid.
Inside's the woman – see her? –
unable to sleep: buried in the hot white pillow
her head feels heavy
like stone.
Round her legs
round her arms
I've twisted a lead-white sheet
like a living person –
and tightened her skin, darkened her veins with blood.
This is the woman's picture. Now you must tell me
whether it's real.

Agnès It's dark.

Boy Then look more closely:
what colour are her eyes?

Agnès Grey – turning black – like my eyes now.

Boy   *Like yours now.*
And her hair? Pay attention.

Agnès Dark – damp – heavy – the weight of mine now.

Boy   *Of your hair now.*

And her mind?

Agnès You've given her my mind – skin – mouth –
voice –

Boy *I've given her your mind – skin – mouth – voice –*
                                        – says the Boy –

Agnès – drawn its exact music.

Boy   *– drawn its exact music.*
And here
under the bone –

Agnès   No.

172

Boy – in the hot space between her ribs –

Agnès   No.

Boy I've painted the woman's heart.

Agnès   No! – not 'the woman' – I am Agnès.
My name's Agnès.

Boy   *Agnès.*

Agnès What use to me is a picture?

Boy   *Agnès.*

Agnès A picture – says Agnès – is nothing.
Love's not a picture: love is an act.

End of Part One.

Part Two

VII THE PROTECTOR'S BAD DREAM

Angels 2 *and* **3** People are saying –

Protector People are saying what?

Angels 2 *and* **3** Saying the book eats –

Protector Saying the book eats what?

Angels 2 *and* **3**   TIME – CORN – RENT.
Say it's a crow eating the seed making the people –

Protector What?

Angels 2 *and* **3**   TALK – LAUGH – STARVE.
Not just the book – say that the Boy –

Protector Say that the Boy what?

Angels 2 *and* **3**   DRAWS – FROM – LIFE.
Say there's a page
where the skin never dries –

Protector Page where the what?

Angels 2 *and* **3**   SKIN – STAYS – DAMP.

Angel 2 Wet like the white
part of an egg –

Angel 3 Wet like a woman's mouth –
wet where a woman screams shrieks
shrieks like a fox
shrieks in the night in a secret bed.

Angel 2 Licking her lips
flicking her tongue
gripping the Boy in a secret bed.

Angels 2 *and* **3**   What kind of man WILL – NOT – SEE?
                    What kind of man WILL – NOT – SEE?

VIII THE PROTECTOR AND AGNÈS

Protector The Protector wakes up
feels in the half-light
for the reassurance of a human body –
puts out his hand to be reassured by a human body –
feels for his wife –
Where is she?

Agnès Here – smiles Agnès – I'm here by the window.
You were thrashing in your sleep. Why?

Protector What is it you're watching?

Agnès Nothing. Sunrise. Plum-trees flowering.
And smoke – why that black smoke in May?

Protector We're burning villages.

Agnès Ah. Why?

Protector To protect the family.

Agnès Ah. Yes. Good. From what?

Protector Don't look.

Agnès And in the meadow I saw a guard reach down
into the buttercups to pick up a baby –

Protector Don't look, Agnès.

Agnès – to pick it up – how odd – on the point of a
stick. Oh and I saw the Boy out riding into the wood like
a picture out of his own book.
Touch me.
Kiss me.
Take my head in your hands.

Protector Don't be a child, Agnès.

Agnès Grip my hair in your fist. Yes.
Put your fingers into my mouth. Yes. Your tongue into my mouth now. Yes. Kiss me.

Protector Only a child, Agnès, asks for a kiss.

Agnès I'm not a child – don't call me a child.

Protector No pure woman asks for a kiss.
No clean woman asks to be touched.
You are. You are a child, Agnès – say it.

Agnès Don't call me a child –

Protector You're a child – say it.

Agnès I refuse to be called a child.

Protector I said to you say it.

Agnès No.

Protector Say it.

Agnès No.

Protector You will say to me 'I am a child'.

Agnès Ask *him* what I am.

Protector Say 'I am a child', Agnès.

Agnès Ask *him* what I am. Go to the wood. Ask *him* –

Protector Ask who?

Agnès – the one who writes on skin – ask him what I am – the Boy.

IX THE PROTECTOR AND THE BOY

Protector He finds the Boy
    sitting against a tree
    looking at his own reflection
    in the blade of a knife.
    Love-sick, thinks the Protector,
    easy to strangle – like a girl.
    What're you doing here?

Boy Nothing.

Protector What is it you're looking at?

Boy Nothing, says the Boy,
    thumbing the knife.

Protector Thinking about?

Boy I'm thinking that when this wood and this light
    are cut through by eight lanes of poured concrete,
    I'm thinking that the two of us
    and everyone we love
    will have been dead for a thousand years.

Protector The future's easy: tell me about now.

Boy Now there's just one slit
    of pink light cut in the sky.

Protector Tell me about now.

Boy Now there's just you me
    and a knife.

Protector Tell me about now:
    who is this woman? –
    the one they say –
    taunt me and say screams out
    from a secret page –
    says screams and sweats with you

in a secret bed?
What is her name?

Boy I thought you trusted me.

Protector What is her name?

Boy I thought you loved me and protected me.

Protector What is this woman's name? Is it Agnès?
Is what? Her name is what?

Boy Not Agnès – no no no no no no no – Marie – her
name's Marie – Marie: her sister.
Look at her.

*Angel 2 appears as Marie, Angel 3 as her husband
John. John is attempting to zip up Marie's dress.*

She came to me. She was bored. She wanted to be Venus.

Marie I'm bored. I want to be Venus. Put me in the
book. Illuminate me.
AH! THAT HURTS!

John Sorry.

Boy Then she wanted to be an angel. She wanted to
crank the universe round on its axis.

Marie Make me an angel. Give me power. I want to
control the universe.

Boy Her marriage was banal. She longed for excitement.

Marie How do I look?

John We're late.

Marie THEN GET ME MY SHOES! NOT THOSE – THE RED
ONES!

Boy She volunteered to be Greed and Luxury – was
happy to let me draw from life sick acts of perversity.

178

Marie Feed me pomegranates and soft-cooked eggs –
roast meat for me and drown me in wine and cream –
wash me in goat-milk – strip me – dress me – strip me
again – toss me naked into the toy-box. Draw my mouth
as a scarlet thread. Shame me – chain me – Drag me to
hell. Shut me in eternal darkness with the devil. I'M
READY!

John I don't want to hear. I don't want to know. Let's
go, Marie. We're late – we're going to be late – let's go.
We're going to be late, let's go, let's go, let's go.

Protector And her husband? –

Boy – was complicit.

*Angels 2 and 3 start to leave. The Boy follows them
off.*

Protector Is this the truth? Is this the truth?

Boy Oh yes – believe me – it's the truth.

They go. The Protector is left alone.

Protector And since this is what the man – this man so
much needed to believe – so he – the man – this man –
believed it.

And that same evening tells his wife – entertains her –
reveals – ha! – how – secretly – the Boy enjoys – guess –
guess – guess – that whore her sister – yes! – and how
that other man – that fool the husband – smiles the
Protector – is complicit.

X AGNÈS AND THE BOY

Agnès Agnès puts on her shoes
steps through the stone slit

179

turns up the stone stairs
slips into the writing-room where the Boy
> him
> yes
> the liar
> look

lifts his head –

Boy Why are you crying?

Agnès You lied to me.

Boy In what way lied?

Agnès All night your voice in my head
wound itself round and around and around and around
my sister.
Her mouth fastened to yours
in a bad dream
and her hair stuck –
stuck like gold-leaf to your skin in a bad dream
and covered your eyes.

Boy What dream?

Agnès My sister – you – the liar – you and my sister.

Boy I lied for you, not to you.

Agnès Prove it.

Boy I lied to protect you.

Agnès Protect – protect – protect:
to protect me or to protect yourself?

Boy This isn't true.

Agnès Prove it.
Let him see. Show him us.

Boy Show him us how?

Agnès Or do you love him too?
  Do you fasten your mouth
  to his mouth too and bite –
  bite on his lip like you bite on mine?

Boy What is it – says the Boy – you want from me?

Agnès While the dead heap up in the meadow
  while human beings burn in the marketplace
  make a new page:
  Push our love into that man's eye
  like a hot needle.
  Blind him with it.
  Make him cry blood.

  End of Part Two.

Part Three

*A long table is spread with pages from the completed
book. The Boy moves along the table explaining the
pictures.*

Boy Here are your enemies
   lined up on a gibbet.

Protector Hanging – excellent – like Judas.

Boy A vine-hook
   cutting a traitor's throat.

Protector Yes yes – and who are these?

Boy These naked boys have dug their own graves –
   they're waiting in an orchard to be shot.

Protector And what are these streaks of light?

Boy A night bombardment:
   Gomorrah – see it? – being turned to dust.

Protector Yes yes, I see it – now show me Paradise.

Boy An aquamarine flash –
   streets running with human fat –

Protector I see it – but show me Paradise.

Boy A carmine flame licking a field of wheat –

Protector I SAID NOW SHOW ME PARADISE.

Boy Ah – ah – ah – no – yes – what? – Paradise?

   But this is Paradise.
   Here is your mill
   and here are your cherry trees.
   Here's – look – Marie shopping in the shopping-mall

and John at the airport collecting air-miles.
This is Paradise.
These are its concrete walls.
And here – with a diamond skull –
the black dog at its gate.

Agnès If this is Paradise – says Agnès –
then where is Hell?

Boy Here – smiles the Boy – it's on this secret page.

Agnès takes the page and looks at it.

Agnès Where are the pictures?

Boy They're here: I've painted them with words.

Agnès What words?

Boy Read them.

Agnès Read? Read? How can a woman read? What
words?
    Is this a word?
    Or this? – this? – this? – or this?
    Where does a word end and another word begin?
    Where are the pictures?
    What use to a woman is a word?

Boy The book is finished.
    My work – smiles the Boy – is done.

The Boy goes.

XII THE PROTECTOR AND AGNÈS

*The Protector examines the page in silence, then begins
to read it to Agnès.*

Protector mouth –
                              – see it –
    mouth

          – writes the Boy –
heart hair mouth nail hand skin blood – her neck
          – writes the Boy –
of amethyst, her long white back,
even the gold-flecked iris of her eye:
each part
each part
each part of her body
          – writes the Boy –
she has offered and has used for her own pleasure.
Like the man
          – writes the Boy –
like the man who bends down the branch in summer –
to cut the most high-up flower
          – writes – writes the Boy –
I have reached up for her love
and have bent her willingly to the ground.
And at her invitation
her own invitation
          – writes the Boy –
we have used and used and used and used
have used each other
as
          – writes the Boy –
pornography.
This
is what the woman
what Agnès
what your wife your property
          – writes the Boy –
what your wife your property
asks me to say to you.

Agnès Ah.
Read it – oh read it again.

Protector Keep away.

Agnès And show me –

Protector Keep away.

Agnès Please show me –

Protector Keep away.

Agnès I want to see.

Protector Cover your arms.
  Cover your face and hair.
  Stitch shut your lips before your pink pink
      flicking tongue
  snakes back into my mouth the way it burrowed
      into his
  NOW KEEP AWAY FROM ME.

Agnès Ah ah ah ah ah ah oh please please
  oh please let me see the word for love.

XIII CHORUS OF ANGELS
AND THE PROTECTOR

Angels 2 *and* 3 Set the earth spinning –
  fill it with iron and stone.

Angel 3 Make a man out of dust.

Angel 2   Good.

Angel 3 Prop him naked on two stick legs.

Angel 2   Good.

Angel 3 Prop him tottering next to a tree.

Angel 2   Good.

Angels 2 *and* 3 Tempt him, taunt him, clothe him, spit
him out.

185

Protector Expel him from joy
  with a lacerating whip.
  Make him sweat, cry,
  scratch at the earth's crust.

Angel 3 Make him jealous – make him ashamed.

Protector Make each man ashamed – yes – to be human.

Protector *and* **Angels 2** *and* **3** Put voices into his mind.

Angel 3 Confront the Boy
                    – says one –
  follow him into the wood.

Angel 2 No
                    – says another voice –
  be wise, be calm, be merciful.

Protector Take his hair in your fist
                    – says the third –
  pull his head back for a kiss:
  and as you are cutting one long clean incision
  through the bone
  examine your own portrait
  in the glass-black mirror of his eyes.

XIV THE PROTECTOR AND AGNÈS

Agnès sits at a long table. In front of her, a metal dish, the lid removed, and a spoon.

Protector Woman and her Protector – night.
  A room. A balcony. A long white table.
  What has he placed in front of her?
  What has he placed in front of her?

Agnès A silver dish.

Protector What does she lift from the silver dish?
  I said what does she lift from the silver dish?

Agnès The warm round silver lid.

Protector What does the woman do now?
I said what does the woman do now?

Agnès I'm not the woman: I'm Agnès.

Protector I said what does the woman do now?

Agnès Eats.

Protector Good. Say it.

Agnès The woman eats.

Protector What makes the woman eat?
I said what makes the woman eat?

Agnès Hunger. Appetite. Her curiosity.

Protector No: her obedience.

Agnès Ah.

Protector Her obedience.

Agnès Ah.

Protector Say it.
I said to you say it.

Agnès Her obedience now makes her eat.

Protector Her obedience to her husband – that is correct –
now makes her eat.
How does it taste – says the man.

Agnès Good, she says – salt and sweet. Why?

Protector Good?

Agnès Yes, she says – good, she says – salt strange and
sweet.
Why?

Protector Good? How is it good?

187

Agnès Sweet as my own milk, yes – good – but salt –
salt as my own tears. Why?

Protector Good? How is it good?

Agnès Why?
What has my husband my Protector given me to eat?

Protector His heart, Agnès.

Agnès What heart?

Protector His heart – the Boy.

*The Protector opens out his hands: they are stained
with blood.*

Agnès No.

Protector His heart – the Boy –

Agnès No – no – nothing –

Protector – his heart – his heart –

Agnès Nothing you can do –

Protector – the Boy – his heart –

Agnès Nothing I ever eat
nothing I drink
will ever take the taste of that Boy's heart
out of this body.

No force you use
nothing you forbid
can take away the pictures that Boy's hands
draw on this skin.

He can unfold the tight green bud
unwrap the tree, darken the wood,
lighten the sky, blacken the dust
with rain – each mark he makes on me is good
each colour clear –

Crush.

Burn.
Break.
Tear.
Put out my eyes.

Hang.
Drown.
Stone.
Stab.
Cut out my tongue.

Nothing
nothing –
not if you strip me to the bone with acid –
will ever take the taste of that Boy's heart
out of this mouth.

XV ANGEL I

Third miniature: the woman falling.
  The Boy reappears as Angel 1.

Angel 1 This – says the Angel – shows the Woman
  Falling:
  here – look – the man takes a knife
  but the woman's quicker, and jumps.
  See how her body has dropped
  from the balcony –
  how I pause her mid-fall –
  at the exact centre of the page.
  Here in the night sky – see them –
  stars hold in a bright web
  her black silhouette on blue.
  As she drops from the house
  three small angels – look –
  are watching her calmly
  from the margin.

In their face in their eyes
see their cold fascination
with human disaster
as they turn from the falling woman to where
the white lines of the Saturday car park cover
the heaped-up dead.

Lessons in Love and Violence

'Then said Jonathan unto David, whatsoever
thy soul desireth, I will do it even for thee'

1 Samuel 20:4

Music
George Benjamin

Text
Martin Crimp

Co-commissioned and co-produced by
The Royal Opera, Covent Garden, London,
Dutch National Opera, Amsterdam,
Hamburg State Opera,
Opéra de Lyon, Lyric Opera of Chicago,
Gran Teatre del Liceu, Barcelona
and Teatro Real Madrid

Lessons in Love and Violence, conducted by the composer, was first performed by The Royal Opera, Covent Garden, at the Royal Opera House, London, on 10 May 2018. The cast was as follows:

King Stéphane Degout
Isabel Barbara Hannigan
Gaveston / Stranger Gyula Orendt
Mortimer Peter Hoare
Boy, *later* **Young King** Samuel Boden
Witness 1 / Singer 1 / Woman 1 Jennifer France
Witness 2 / Singer 2 / Woman 2 Krisztina Szabó
Witness 3 / Madman Andri Björn Robertsson

Stage Direction Katie Mitchell
Sets and Costumes Vicki Mortimer
Lighting Director James Farncombe
Movement Director Joseph Alford

Characters

King
baritone

Isabel, *his wife*
soprano

Gaveston
his advisor and intimate friend
doubling as
Stranger
baritone

Mortimer
his chief military expert
tenor

Boy, *later* **Young King**
an adolescent, son of Isabel and King
high tenor / haute-contre

Witness 1 / Singer 1 / Woman 1
high (coloratura) soprano

Witness 2 / Singer 2 / Woman 2
mezzo-soprano

Witness 3 / Madman
bass-baritone

Also required (all silent roles)

Young Girl, *daughter of Isabel and King*
Other Witnesses
Audience at Play, *to a maximum of, say, twenty*

Part One

SCENE ONE

Palace: King's Apartments.
King, Mortimer, Gaveston, Isabel, the Boy and Girl.

Mortimer
It's nothing to do with loving a man. It's love full stop that is poison. The whole human body –

King
Yes – we hear you – love full stop –

Mortimer
And the money –

King
Always the money – always the human body –

Mortimer
– the money you spend –

King
– we will spend whatever we like –

Mortimer
The money you spend with Gaveston while people starve is unacceptable –

King
– Ah – ah – 'with Gaveston' – 'unacceptable' –

Mortimer
– yes when the price of bread –

King
Don't bore me with the price of bread.
Don't block my mind with politics.

Mortimer
You are the king.

King
Then treat me – Mortimer – as king.
Love me. Defer to me.
Defer to my friend and advisor Gaveston.
Let us spend money on poetry and music.
Or would you rather we preferred for our entertainment
human blood and the machinery of killing?

Mortimer
No one is talking about blood.

King
Oh? What? No one? –

Mortimer
Nor do I fight wars for my entertainment –

King
– Who is no one? Am I no one? –

Mortimer
– I fight to protect our people –

King
– I thought I was king.
Who am I, Gaveston? – tell me.

Gaveston
King – you are king.

King
King – I am king.
Don't call me no one, Mortimer.
Don't go out into the world and call love poison.
Love makes us human.

Mortimer
So does the need to kill.
So – forgive me – does politics.

King
Do you want – Mortimer – to be me? –

Mortimer
I don't understand.

King
– want to be me –
take my wife – Mortimer –
use my bed – Mortimer –
murder and kill and take my crown?
Because cities will burn and wherever you touch the
immaculate surface of her skin your politics will
leave streaks of my blood.
But maybe – tell me – does Mortimer keep a cat?

Takes Girl on his lap.

They say there's an insane person claiming to be king
on evidence provided by his cat.
Maybe his name is Mortimer.

Mortimer
I am loyal.

King
What did he say?

Gaveston
He said he is loyal.
He claims not to have
a cat.

King
He tells me my people are starving – but who have
I ever harmed?

Isabel
No one. Yourself – sometimes.

King
Not you?

Isabel
Never.

King
You see: I am entirely innocent.
And have I hurt Gaveston?

Isabel
Ask Gaveston.

King
Have I hurt you, Gaveston?

Gaveston turns away.

I ASKED YOU A QUESTION ANSWER ME.

Gaveston
Not when you grip my neck.
Not when you hold my right hand deliberately over
  a flame.
Not even when you have forced me to swim in winter
   under the dull grey ice till my lungs are beginning
  to split –
Oh but when you let that man
equate money with love and the whole human body
with shame and bitterness –
when he questions your right to be king –
when his eyes move – look – like a sly animal's over
  everything you own
then I want to run at his throat with a steel razor –
Take his property.

Mortimer
No – none of this is true.

Gaveston
Take Mortimer's property.
Take his house – take over his land. Punish him.
Give me his rents.
Remove from his finger that fat gold ring.

Mortimer
> None of this is true.

Isabel
> But Mortimer is our friend –

King
> Yes Mortimer is our friend –

Gaveston
> Mortimer – Mortimer – even the name means death –

King
> Mortimer is our friend
> and is loyal and in his own cold way – believe me –
> Mortimer loves each one of us.

Gaveston
> Then why in his own cold way when I take my hand
> and I place it here –
> place it like this –

> *He takes the King by the throat perhaps – a gesture*
> *that suggests both violence and intimacy.*

>   – does he feel –
> look at his face –
> disgust?
> Tell me I'm wrong – dead man Mortimer.

Isabel
> Tell him he's wrong.

> *Mortimer looks away.*

King
> Oh my poor friend Mortimer –
> from this moment you have no land –
> from today you will have no property.
> The clothes you are wearing
> you no longer own.
> And being now nothing
> you have no name.

Isabel
Don't call him nothing.

King
I say that he has no name:
do not contradict me, Isabel.
I say he is nothing.
I say that all I can see where Mortimer once stood
is the black space of a collapsing star.

Gaveston
But I see the ring.

King (*to Boy*)
Ah. Sweetheart.

Boy
What is it
Daddy?

King
Bring Gaveston the ring.

Mortimer is impassive. The Boy struggles to remove the ring.

Gaveston
The boy needs a knife.

Isabel
No!

King
No violence please.
Let ours be a regiment
of tolerance and love.

SCENE TWO

Palace: Isabel's Apartments, some months later.
Isabel, Mortimer, the Boy and Girl, and a number of
Witnesses.

Isabel

Who are these people, Mortimer?
They're frightening my children.

Mortimer

I've travelled, Isabel.
I wanted to see my country.
I began in the mountains
but there was nothing to eat but stone.
So I came down to the spring meadow
but in each refuge
I found a shepherd with his throat cut
and the clean bones of animals.
In the foothills
I dug for roots
and lay for heat
in the ash of burnt villages – but –
closer – Isabel – to our own city
I found these witnesses.
And led them in secret
here – Isabel – to your door.

Isabel

Why?

Mortimer

Listen.

Isabel

What is it she's holding?

Witness 2

My husband died – forgive me –
in your husband's war –

but then your husband gave our land –
he gave away our home – he gave our property –
to Gaveston.
I came here with nothing but my body
and sold it over and over – forgive me.
I had a baby – oh forgive me – but my baby died
and this is my baby's ash.
Since Gaveston has taken everything
then I would like him to take my baby too.
Yes – yes – here is my baby too. Take it.

Isabel

Keep her away – I am not Gaveston.
My name's not Gaveston – keep her away from me.

Witness 1

They say one jewel from Gaveston's silver cup –
one cut emerald –
could've fed my whole dead family –

Witness 2

They say he's magic and can predict the future.
I hope his future
is to be burned alive.

Witness 1

They say one night of the music
for that man Gaveston –

Isabel

'They say' – 'they say' – that's not a witness –

Witness 1

– say just one night costs the same
as one whole year of our labour –

Isabel

No there is no connection –

Witness 1

– one whole year of work –

Isabel
– no connection between our music and your labour.

Mortimer
Tell her what else the people say.

Witness 3
They say
we know why
the poor sleep three
in a bed but
why do
the rich?

Isabel (*to Girl*)
Bring me a cup of vinegar.

Pause.

Listen – witnesses – I respect each one of you.
I am a human being and a mother too.
My body is forked like yours:
it loves – and breaks –
like a common criminal's –
with the same pain.
But do not come here
trying to put a price on music.

She takes the cup of vinegar from the Girl.

This – is acid –
and this pearl . . .

She takes a pearl from around her neck.

. . . this pearl – you are right –
would buy each one of you a house with fourteen
    rooms
and beds and winter firewood but –
the beauty of the pearl

is not what the pearl can buy.
The beauty of the pearl – like the slow radiance
    of music –
is what the pearl is.
Look.

She drops the pearl into the vinegar.

Fourteen rooms dissolve.
And the whole winter stock of wood.
The dull dreams of the average dreamer –
money – property – burn away
in the acid of   of   of
of pure and inexchangeable value.
And? – what? – which one of you will drink it?
Maybe this one – this one – you – you – three in a bed –
the slanderer!

She tries to force Witness 3 to drink.
    Mortimer grabs her and knocks away the cup.

Now give them all money and get them all out.

The Witnesses go.

Boy
    Why do the poor sleep
    three in a bed – Mummy?

Isabel
    To keep warm – sweetheart.

Boy
    And why – Mummy – do the rich?

Isabel
    The man told a lie – sweetheart.

Boy
    Why did the man tell a lie?
    Why did the man tell a lie – Mummy?

Isabel

Because he is poor and angry.
Mortimer – tell me – what is it like to kill?

Mortimer

There is an art to killing – but no joy.

Isabel

What is it I should do?

Mortimer

Provide an entertainment.
Empty Gaveston's mind with music –
and I can destroy him.

Isabel

No one must harm my husband.

Mortimer

No one will harm your husband –
only Gaveston.
What are you thinking, Isabel?

Isabel

Move away.
The children are watching us.

SCENE THREE

Palace: a theatre.
The theatre's curtain is closed – empty chairs are set
out for an audience.
King and Gaveston.
Later, Isabel, the Children, Singers 1 and 2, Mortimer.
King seizes Gaveston by the wrist.

King

How can I love you?
A man with the steel hand
and sleepy smile of an assassin.

Gaveston
>Yes I'm a human razor:
>take care or I'll cut your throat.

King
>You bite your fingernails like a boy does –
>the skin's broken where you punched the wall –
>why did you punch the wall?

Gaveston
>Love is a prison:
>I wanted to see daylight.

King
>How can I love a man who calls love a prison? –
>who says he would cut my throat?
>How would you kill me, Gaveston? –
>would it be slow? –
>or sudden?

Gaveston
>I'd only kill you for money.

King
>For money? – kill me for money? –
>   how much money?

Gaveston
>How much would you pay me?

King
>How long will it take to die? – I'll pay you for every
>   minute.
>Tell me my future, Gaveston.

Gaveston
>Then open your hand.

>*King opens his hand.*

King
>What can you see?

Pause.

Gaveston
Here – look – is my baby king.
He appoints ministers and sets villages alight
even in his painted cradle –
and his rattle is a box of emeralds.
And here –
    – keep it still –
        – is his child bride Isabel.
This same hand that now seals the instruction
to sever a man's head
strips bare her silk body.
Now your belovèd boy's torn out of her –
and another child –
and this – look – shows how the children grow
so fast does life move till already this line cutting
    across
means war or fire or storm or crops burning –

King
Yes yes politics – but where –

Gaveston
– means Mortimer testing for Isabel
the machinery of killing –

King
    – Mortimer – machinery –
but where is my future? –
where is my brother Gaveston?

Gaveston
You know where I am:
inside your life.
I've no life out of it.
I live where you are looking:
in the hard palm of your hand.

Isabel enters with the two children.

*Behind them, the audience for the performance,
who come and sit in the chairs.*

Isabel
Please everyone – be seated.

Gaveston
What is the music, Isabel?

Isabel
The killing of Saul
and of Jonathan his son.

Gaveston
I don't like killing – neither will your children.

Isabel
A child knows it's normal to kill our enemies –
but this will be David's lament: there is no violence.

*King has taken his place in front row of the audience,
with his children beside him.*

Gaveston
I have no enemies.

Isabel
Please – sit next to me.

Gaveston
Won't you sit with your husband.

Isabel
I am closer to my husband
Gaveston
the closer I am to you.

*As they sit together in the back row of the audience,
the onstage curtain goes up to reveal two female
Singers, exquisitely dressed.*

Singers
And David said:

where is my brother?
where is my brother Jonathan?
'They fastened his body'
– said the messenger –
'to the wall of Beth-shan.'
Where is my brother?
where is my brother Jonathan?

Gaveston
Oh how very beautifully they sing –

Isabel
You have tears in your eyes –

Singers
They took down his body to be burned.

Isabel
– is it too tight?

Gaveston
Is what?

Isabel
The ring, the ring –
is Mortimer's ring too tight for your finger?
Don't move away from me – no –
sit close sit close to me Gaveston sit closer –

Singers
And David said:
where is my brother?
oh where is my brother Jonathan?

But Gaveston stands when he sees Mortimer staring at him from the edge of the space. Members of the onstage audience stand around him as if to block an escape. The Singers continue.

Gaveston
Dead man Mortimer –

what've you come to tell me, dead man Mortimer? –
the price of butter? – or is it the price of bread?

Mortimer
I've come for my property.

Gaveston
Oh? Oh? Property? Here's your property.
Take her.

*He pushes Isabel towards Mortimer. Now the King
notices the disturbance.*

Singers
Where is my brother Jonathan?

King
Arrest this man. Stop the song. Stop the music.
I SAID STOP THE MUSIC NOW!

The onstage Singers stop.

I order the arrest of Mortimer.

No one moves.

I command you to listen to your king.

No one moves.

I command you to kneel down at my feet
and swear to me your obedience.

No one moves.

NO BUT YOU WILL SPARE ME GAVESTON.

SCENE FOUR

*Palace: private apartment
The King alone, holding a letter.
Isabel enters.*

Isabel
    I'm cold.
    I was dreaming.
    Come and sleep.

King
    I never sleep.

Isabel
    I'm cold. Come and hold me.

King (*reads*)
    'And one man drove a sword
    through his body
    and another
    beheaded him in a ditch.'

Isabel
    You're tired: come and sleep.

King
    I couldn't save him.
    I couldn't save him, Isabel.

Isabel
    Stop now. Come and sleep.

King
    Who have I ever harmed?

Isabel
    I'm cold. Even my lips are cold. Why are my lips
      so cold?
    Won't you kiss me?

King
    I could hold his hand –
    like this –
    steady like this – Isabel –
    over a flame
    and he would meet my eyes while his hand burned
      and burned over that same flame
    and smile.

Isabel

Ah.

Isabel turns away from him.

Why should you love him – tell me –
still love him – tell me – whom all the world hates?

King

Because he loved me more than all the world.
But why have you turned away?

Isabel

Turned away?

King

Turned to the dark – yes – turned away from me.

Isabel

How have I turned to the dark?

King

To hide your face there in the dark.

Isabel

I haven't turned to the dark.

King

Then show me your face.

Isabel

No.

King

Show me your eyes.

Isabel

No.

King

Isabel!

She turns back to him.

Isabel

Here is my face.
And here – look – are my tears.
What have I ever hidden?
No part of this body.
No part of my mind – not my opinions.
Not ever my love.
I'm not the one, my poor poor sweetheart
who has turned and turned
and keeps on deliberately turning to the dark.

King

I will break him.
I will break Mortimer open.
I will cut his living body into four –

Isabel

I am taking our son –

King

– will hunt out each associate of his crime –

Isabel

I am taking our son –

King

– smoke them out of their own homes –
drown whole cities in their blood –

Isabel

I said I am taking our son to Mortimer.
Only he can protect him. (*Pause.*) Don't you see?

No reaction from the King.

Then stay in the dark.
Play king alone here in the dark.
We will leave you the box of toys.

She goes.

After a long pause, King goes back to the letter.

King (*reads*)
'But he mocked them
and asked by whose authority he should die.
They said: that of Mortimer.
And Gaveston replied:
"Mortimer is a dog.
His snout is between the queen's legs
and his breath smells of murder."
So they bound his hands.
And one man drove a sword through his body
and . . .
and another . . .'

He breaks off, unable to go on reading.

Part Two

Mortimer's house.
Mortimer, Isabel and Boy. Later, the Madman.
The Girl is skipping.

Mortimer
D'you like dogs?
I'll buy you a dog.
Or maybe you'd like a lion?
Would you like to be king
and keep lions?

Boy
My father
is king

Mortimer
Your father cannot be king –
he wants you to take his place.

Boy
I'm a boy.
I have no experience.

Mortimer
Your mother and I will advise you.

Boy
What kind of dog?

Isabel
A greyhound –

Mortimer
– yes an immaculate greyhound.
But first you must show us
you understand justice and can protect the people.

Boy
Oh?

Mortimer
Yes from decadence and terror. Let the man in.

Madman comes in.

This man is promoting revolution.
He claims to be king.

Madman
No not a claim but a totally true statement.

Isabel
Tell my son what it is you believe.

Madman
I believe I am king and demand to be heard.

Mortimer
Oh he demands. Test him.

Boy
What is your evidence?

Madman
I am told I am king not only by inheritance but by the will of the universe encoded in a bright pattern of stars.

Mortimer
Test him. Who told him?

Boy
Who told you you are king?

Madman
I was told by Felicity.

Boy
Who is Felicity?

Madman
Felicity has green eyes. Felicity is a cat.

Mortimer
Test him. I said you must test him.

Boy
My father is king.
And I will be king after him.
To claim to be king is – oh – don't you see? –
unintelligent.

Mortimer
No – is a crime. Say it.

Boy
Is a crime.

Madman
No not a crime but a totally true statement.

Mortimer
And to make this claim
is to ask to be put to death. Say it.

Boy
But his mind's not right.

Mortimer
Say it –

Isabel
– we need you to say it.

Madman
No I am of totally sound mind and I will destroy
this child and rule with my cat in perpetual glory.

Isabel
He says he'll destroy you.

Boy
But his mind's not right. Mortimer – spare him.

Madman

I don't ask to be spared I ask you to offer me
respect and obedience.

Mortimer (*taking the Girl's skipping rope*)
We can offer you this rope.

Boy

No!

Madman

No not rope but respect and –

Boy

Be merciful!

*Mortimer begins to strangle the Madman with the
skipping rope.*

Mortimer

Let one poisonous idea leak out into the world
and the whole world will be contaminated.
Look.
I said look at this clearly and learn.

*Boy tries to bury his face in Isabel but Isabel –
although disturbed – forces him to look.*

Understand –
that when you are king –
there will be no room for one man's love for another –
no room for madness –
or for disorder inside –
the machinery of the regulated world.

Madman dies.

Boy

Ah.
But mercy . . .

Mortimer
When a man will be cut into pieces and burned
a rope is mercy.

Boy
What kind of crown
will I have?

Mortimer
Your father's true crown of gold.

Boy
Where is my father? –

Mortimer
Your father is safe.

Boy
– is he in prison?

Isabel
Take your sister into the garden please
and pick her a sweet apple.

The children go out.

Tell me: how will you take the crown?

Mortimer
In front of witnesses. By logical argument.

Isabel
And after that?
I said: and after that?
What are you, Mortimer?

Mortimer
I am a man.

Isabel
Then touch me.

SCENE SIX

Prison.
King, Mortimer, Witnesses.
Later, the Stranger.

King
Drumming – I can hear drumming.
What is it you want from me?

Mortimer
The crown.

King
Drumming – I can hear drumming.

Mortimer
Give me the crown and your son will be king.

King
Drumming – I can hear drumming.

Mortimer
Your son has been chosen king –

King (*mocking*)
    My son has been chosen –

Mortimer
He needs the crown.

King
    – and needs the crown.
Then show me my son.
Let me speak to my children!
Drumming – I can hear drumming.

Mortimer (*to Witnesses*)
Write this down:
he is unfit to rule.
Write he imagines drumming.

King
Oh – I am a bad person.
Oh I have turned to the dark –
And the man I chose as brother –
I could not save –
write that I could not save him –

Mortimer
Self-pity. Write nothing. The crown.

King
Yes I have let my own people starve –
have wept to exquisite music –

Mortimer
The crown –

King
– while the hay lay drowned.

Mortimer
– in front of these witnesses – the crown –

King
Yes I have broken my own country's back
but I will never never let you
dead man Mortimer
take this crown.

King seizes Mortimer's wrist.

What's your opinion now
of the human body?
You and my wife –
are you a good fit?
When your tongue's inside her
– Mortimer –
can you still taste the husband?

Mortimer frees himself.

Mortimer
Write – write this down –

that lechery –
that sodomy –
have decayed his mind.
That he degrades his own wife –
betrays his own son –
so the crown will pass out of his family
and never return.
Write what he said.
Write he is no one.

King
I am not no one.

Mortimer
Write that instead of a man this man has chosen to
be nothing.

Mortimer makes to go.

King
Take it.
Take it, Mortimer – and commend me to my son.

Mortimer takes the crown and leaves with Witnesses.
Two Women remain.
Pause.

What do you want from me?

Women 1 *and* **2**
There is a man waiting.

King
What man?

Women 1 *and* **2**
He comes from Mortimer.
He brings you light.

King
Brings me what light?

Women 1 *and* **2**
What shall we say to him?

King
Say to come in.

Stranger appears.

Women 1 *and* **2**
This is the man.

King
Come forward into the light.
I know you've come to murder me.
Tell me your name.

Stranger
I am a person all the world hates.
I stand outside every door:
no one invites me in.
When pear-blossom opens in spring
I nod to the drum –
hum to the wooden flute:
but no one invites me to dance
on the green meadow.

King
Come forward into the light.

Stranger
Like you I'm king of a stone palace –

King
Tell me your name.

Stranger
          – and like you I am always alone.
You know my name.

Stranger steps into the light.

King (*without expression*)
Gaveston –

225

Stranger
My name is not Gaveston –

King
I know you've been sent to murder me –

Stranger
My name is not Gaveston –

King
– will it be slow? – or sudden? –

Stranger
– you know my name.

King
Tell me my future –

Stranger
You know what my name is –

King
– how will I die? –

Stranger
– open your hand.

Stranger takes the King's hand.
Pause.

Here – look – is the living king.
Naked in his cradle
he rattles the wood frame
and the world – oh the world comes running.
See how the whole line of his life
is tense with pleasure
as Fate unwinds from its oiled machine
one long silk thread –

King
But how will I die?

Stranger

– until here – look – the machinery spits blood –

King

I said how will I die?

Stranger

His wife cries out in the night for Mortimer.

King

I said tell me – tell me –

Stranger

His own child staggers up onto the throne now
as puppet-king and takes his own place
on the puppet-stage of History.

King

– how am I going to die?

Stranger

How?
Don't you see:
The thread is already broken.
You are already dead.

King

No.

Long pause.

Why do I feel nothing?

Stranger

The dead can't feel.

King

No.
Why is my mind blank?

Stranger

The dead
have no thoughts.

King
No. When
did I die?

Stranger
When
means nothing.

King
And how?
Was it murder?

Stranger
Murder – murder
means nothing.

King
No.
Make me feel.

Stranger
I can't.

King
No.
Make me alive again.

Stranger
I can't.

King
Hold my body over the fire
Gaveston.
Make me alive.

Stranger
My name
is not Gaveston.

King
Bind me to a metal rack.
Burn me.
Make me alive.

Stranger
> The dead
> cannot burn.

King
> Love me.
> Burn me.
> Make me alive.

Stranger
> The dead
> cannot love.

King
> Love me.
> Bind me to a rack of hot metal.
> Hold me –
> burn me forever
> in a crucible of fire.

SCENE SEVEN

Palace: a theatre.
*   The theatre as before, its curtain closed, and rows of*
empty chairs.
*   Isabel and the Boy – who is now the Young King –*
both in mourning.
*   Later, the audience.*

Isabel
> What is the music?

Young King
> I have forbidden music.

Isabel
> Then what is behind the curtain?

Young King
　It is
　an entertainment.

Isabel
　Ah.

　Pause.

　Who will be invited to the entertainment?

Young King
　Yes.
　Who shall we invite?
　My father?

Isabel
　Don't play.

Young King
　This is not play.

Isabel
　You're a child.

Young King
　No I am king.

Isabel
　What is behind the curtain?

Young King
　What do you want, Mummy, to be behind the curtain?

Isabel
　Oh –
　a low summer moon.
　Your father – my innocence.

Young King
　My father's dead.
　On no side of this curtain

Mummy
are we innocent.

Short pause.

Let me explain to you
the entertainment.
In a deep pit
under the earth
a man and a woman
murder a king.
On the vacant throne
to gratify the people
they install the woman's child
and plan to conceal the murder –

Isabel
No – where is Mortimer?

Young King
– but from under the earth
echoes and echoes out
the king his father's agony.
The child learns –

Isabel
– I said to you where is Mortimer? –

Young King
– and offers dead man Mortimer no mercy.

*An audience files on silently to sit facing the closed
curtain.*

The name of his crime
Mummy
is cut
into his body –

Isabel
No – stop – spare him –

Young King
– and – when he has read its name –
Mummy –

Isabel
– no – spare him –

Young King
– we cut out his eyes.

The onstage audience have settled into their seats.

With a scene then of a human being
broken and broken
by the rational application
of human justice
our entertainment begins.